ADVERTISING TO CHILDREN IN CHINA

Advertising to Children
in China

Kara Chan and James U. McNeal

The Chinese University Press

Advertising to Children in China
  By Kara Chan and James U. McNeal

© **The Chinese University of Hong Kong**, 2004

ISBN 962–996–142–3 (Hardcover)
ISBN 962–996–179–2 (Paperback)

THE CHINESE UNIVERSITY PRESS
The Chinese University of Hong Kong
SHA TIN, N.T., HONG KONG
Fax: +852 2603 6692
     +852 2603 7355
E-mail: cup@cuhk.edu.hk
Web-site: www.chineseupress.com

Printed in Hong Kong

Table of Contents

List of Tables, Figures & Appendices

Tables

Plate 1: Children marching off to McDonald's

Plate 2: A boy with a five-yuan note at a ship model store

Plate 3: Shows all three markets: primary, influence and future markets

Chapter 1

Children as Consumers in China

As the title of this book suggests, *advertising* is routinely being targeted to *children* in *China*. For the most part it is relatively new but growing at a rapid pace; as far as we know, faster than in any other heavily populated country. Why? In simple terms, children in China now constitute a market, and advertising is one of the main means used to communicate to that market about products and services and their sellers. Marketers who do the advertising use a simple formula to decide what markets to target: People × Money = Markets. That is, the number of *people* in a certain group such as those of the same age, gender, education, or race, multiplied by their income, spending, or economic power measured in *money*, equals one or more *markets*. A market, as we are using the term here, refers to a group of people with money to spend and a willingness to spend it to satisfy their needs. It should be noted that these two principal elements of a market — people and money — drive all business and all business functions including advertising. Let us briefly examine these two factors, that when combined, constitute what is usually called the kids market. (We will use the terms, kids, toddlers, children, tweens, and teens, to represent this market segment in order to reduce reading boredom and also to refer to specific age groups.)

People

At the time of this writing China is the most populated country in the world, and it also holds the largest population of children in the world. Being such a large population in a country with a still-developing infrastructure and communications system, we doubt if the Chinese government or anyone knows precisely how many people there are. But, the figures we use here are the most reliable ones we know of and are gathered by the Population Reference Bureau that regularly tracks world populations. Accordingly, in 2001, which we will refer to as current, there were 1.28 billion people in Mainland China — the geographical topic of most of the writing in this book (Population Reference Bureau, 2003). There is a term, Greater China, that also embraces Macau, Hong Kong, and Taiwan. We will discuss these other entities from time to time, but do not include them in our use of the term, China, to represent Mainland China. Of this nearly 1.3 billion, 23%, or around 300 million are youth under age 15. And of this 300 million youths, 36%, or 108 million, are urban, while over 191 million are rural. We will round off these latter two figures for writing purposes to 100 million children that live in the urban areas of China; 200 million in the rural areas. It is the 100 million kids that are living in the cities where the household incomes are much higher that are the chief interests of marketers and advertisers. These cities largely are located in the Eastern half of China. And it is these Eastern cities that not only have the most concentration of population and wealth, but the most developed infrastructure. Thus, they are the primary focus of mass marketers from Asia, mainly Japan, Korea, Singapore, Hong Kong, and from Western countries such as the United Kingdom and the United States that are looking to expand their product markets.

❑ *One-child policy*

There is another very important characteristic of China's children that logically gives them even more market potential than that of children in other parts of the world. There is usually only *one* of them per family. As a step toward population control China passed a law in 1979 limiting families to one child. Today, one is the standard, particularly in the urban areas. In the Chinese culture it is hoped that the one child is a boy since the male child must assume responsibility for the family when he is grown. Through various selection procedures Chinese families have increased their chances of having a male child. In 1990 there were 111 boys born per 100 girls; today the national average is 117 with some provinces approaching 144, according to a recent *New York Times* article quoting the official New China News Agency and the Population

Reference Bureau (Eckholm, 2002). (The world average is 106.) So, this one child, preferably a boy, holds much more power than just the only-child in the typical family. He or she is born with responsibility, and whatever it takes to grow this child into the head of the household that assumes the family name — currently the girl does not — that will be done — education, health, money, things. So, in virtually all urban families in China there is just one child who probably determines most of the direction and behavior of the household including its consumption patterns. His or her control of the household is so great that this child is often referred to as a "spoiled brat," or in a slightly nicer tone, a "little emperor" (Shao and Herbig, 1994). These only-children receive most of the love and attention of the parents as well as perhaps four grandparents some of whom may live in the same household with the child. In effect, there is a 4-2-1 indulgence factor operating in China — four grandparents and two parents indulging one child. Or what has also been termed the "six pocket syndrome," to refer directly to the children's spending power (Goll, 1995). The net result, which is of great importance to marketers and advertisers, is that the child, at least as much as any one parent, has a substantial say-so in what the household buys and consumes. Rather than the father being in charge of the household, that is, a patriarchy which has historically been the norm in China, or the mother having central control, referred to as a matriarchy, which is common to Western countries, the child is in charge, in which case the family may be termed a "*filiarchy*" (McNeal, 1999).

Money

❏ *Children's influence on household purchases*

Because the only-child is usually the focal point of Chinese families he/she has a great deal of influence on what is bought by the family members for the household. Thus, the child has much market potential because he or she directs much of the family spending. In fact, one study by McNeal and Yeh (1997) estimates that Chinese children influence 68 percent of household purchases (as compared, for example, with around 45 percent for households in the United States). Research shows that this influence extends to many every-day purchased products and services including those consumed in leisure-time behavior of the family such as television viewing, video game playing, shopping, vacations, visits to parks, visits to relatives, and visits to restaurants. Table 1-1 shows a list of products and the degree of children's influence on them by age according to the investigation by McNeal and Yeh (1997). The reader can see that the children's influence covers quite a few products, and

Table 1-1: Chinese children's percent of influence on parents' purchases by age

Item	Age								
	4	5	6	7	8	9	10	11	12
Bakery items	95	95	95	95	94	94	92	89	84
Books	58	59	63	57	57	84	59	71	59
Bread	65	76	61	61	58	61	59	56	65
Candy	88	82	79	79	74	76	70	78	79
Clothing	80	82	84	88	88	88	89	90	90
Cookies	72	68	58	56	60	71	59	58	69
Deli items	35	45	46	48	48	46	48	43	43
Fruits	89	91	91	92	92	93	93	93	93
Fruit juices	89	89	91	92	92	93	93	93	93
Gum	91	93	90	91	91	88	76	83	84
Hair care items	59	59	61	29	30	46	43	53	55
Ice cream	93	94	95	95	95	93	90	88	88
Imported candy	98	98	98	97	97	96	95	95	94
Meats	48	28	37	35	35	38	36	39	35
Milk	71	74	64	70	74	71	60	62	63
Movies	74	98	94	92	90	95	93	93	90
Nuts	92	92	90	90	90	91	91	90	88
Seafood	52	48	51	39	39	60	51	53	50
Soft drinks	71	72	74	73	73	76	68	73	76
Shoes	79	81	60	74	74	82	78	83	75
Stationery	66	62	80	82	88	87	86	85	86
Toothpaste/brush	63	63	61	64	64	75	75	75	76
Toys	93	93	92	92	90	91	90	86	86
Vegetables	38	28	28	18	18	26	28	27	26
Video games	73	98	94	92	90	95	93	93	94

Note: Table reads that 4-year-olds, for example, determine 95 percent of bakery items purchased.

ranges between a low of around 25 percent for vegetables to over 90 percent for bakery items. Moreover, it is apparent from these figures that children's influence is substantial across all ages. For example, four-year-olds influence 98 percent of the household's purchase of imported candy while 12-year-olds determine 90 percent of the purchases of their clothes. Actually, the data in Table 1-1 may be misleading since they suggest that children's influence on household purchases begins at age four. In conversations with Chinese mothers in the cities of Beijing and Tianjin it was learned that their children directly influence some of their purchases by the time the children can utter a few words — somewhere around the age of 18–24 months, much like the toddlers in the United States and in the United Kingdom.

In another study, which examined Chinese children's influence on family weekend leisure-time, the parents were asked to estimate their children's influence on leisure time activities (McNeal and Ji, 1996). These results are shown in Table 1-2 and also represent a wide range of

Table 1-2: Places families may visit on leisure time and degree of children's influence

Places	Influence (%)
Stationery store	72.5
Amusement park	72.4
Zoo	72.2
McDonald's	71.6
Park	70.7
Kentucky's	69.8
Book store	67.7
Toy store	67.3
Grandparents	65.9
Museum	63.7
Food store	58.2
Cinema	50.2
Other restaurant	49.4
Relatives	47.1
Supermarket	40.1
Friend's home	37.8
Clothing store	28.5

household purchases. For example, children determined family visits to amusement parks, zoos, and McDonald's almost three-quarters of the time. And of the 17 destinations listed in Table 1-2, children determine over 50 percent of visits to 12 of them.

In addition to these estimates by the parents of their children's influence on family leisure time activities, their children were asked to "draw what comes to your mind when you think about the long weekend" (a two-day weekend) in order to obtain their thoughts about how they wish to spend their leisure time. (A popular means of revealing what children know and think is to ask them to draw since verbalization is often difficult for them.) One of the drawings from the study is shown in Plate 1 and is characteristic of a number of them. The third-grader shows him and some pals marching off to McDonald's on a Saturday morning in their athletic clothes. Notice, too, that there are grassy areas in the park on the other side of the fence where the children like to play — grass is in short supply in Beijing as it is in most major cities — suggesting that they will play there. But they will move on to McDonald's, as shown, because they will ask their parents to take them there, or better yet, as in this case, ask for money to go there — to partake of the fun, food, and family atmosphere offered by this restaurant chain. Thus, from the results of this qualitative drawing study among the children regarding their thoughts about what activities they prefer for leisure time, and the quantitative study among the parents to ascertain their children's actual input into family activities during leisure time, we can see that the children are major determinants of the time and money Chinese families devote to leisure activities.

Overall, it has been estimated that children in only the large cities of China exert direct influence annually on family purchases of over US$60 billion per year (McNeal and Zhang, 2000). This includes US$50 billion of food and beverages, US$5 billion on children's clothing, US$3 billion for school supplies, and about US$3 billion for play items. Given that household purchasing power (GDP) is growing rapidly in China — it was approximately US$1,520 in 1990; around US$4,600 in 2002 (Population Reference Bureau, 2003) — it can be expected that children's influence on household spending will grow commensurately. (In the United States, and in most of the Western nations, increases in children's influence on family spending outpace increases in household income.) Therefore, the estimates presented here are considered conservative. It should be emphasized that these estimates are for *direct* influence only, that is, where the children actually make requests for the goods and services. They do not include the *indirect*, or passive influence in which parents buy what they believe their children like without being asked. This latter figure has not been estimated for Chinese children, but it is believed that it is larger than the direct influence measure (as it is in Western nations). Thus, the combined direct and indirect influence of children, ages 2–14, on household spending in urban China approximates US$125 billion.

Chinese children's influence on mom's spending can be seen and heard through observation research conducted at the point-of-purchase, that is, in stores, in the street markets, at kiosks located in tourist attractions and local parks. In these places, in the presence of products, the children often ask for snack items, play items, and almost always, school items. And sometimes they will do more than ask; they will demand, seemingly knowing the exact amount of pressure it takes to get mom to acquiesce. For example, children often assert their authority ceded to them by the family in major department stores where Chinese shoppers can find most of the goods and services sought — from foods in the basement to children's clothes on the fifth or sixth floor, and in-between, clothing for mom and dad, and appliances and furnishings for the home. At the beginning of each set of stairs or escalators in most department stores there is a refreshment kiosk offering ice cream, frozen treats, and many beverages. It is here, particularly, that the children can be observed expressing their wants; later again in the kids' clothing department, again in the stationery floor, and of course in the basement supermarket. And even before the parents arrive at the department store, often before they even leave for the department store, children usually have made requests including, "Let's stop at McDonald's!" One Beijing mother told us that while she and her six-year-old daughter are bicycling to the marketplace the girl is making frequent requests such as, "Can we get some more writing paper?" and "Can we look at sweaters?"

Research shows that there are some differences in children's requests by gender, with girls often asking for more bakery items, fruit juices, ice cream, and toys than boys do. Also, girls tend to ask grandparents who live with them for more clothing items while boys ask for more school items and video games (McNeal and Yeh, 1997).

Research also reveals that children may view their grandparents who live with them as another "source of supply." For example, 43 percent of Chinese kids studied ask grandparents for books, 35 percent for toys, 28 percent for vegetables, and 23 percent request school supplies (McNeal and Yeh, 1997). Increasingly, mom and dad are both working in China, and working longer hours (McNeal and Yeh, 2003). Consequently, grandparents who tend their grandchildren actually solicit requests from them, particularly for food items.

As will be discussed in the next chapter, children learn about new products from other children, advertising, and store visits. When convenient they make requests for these products to their parents. Parents recognize that the children know about some products such as computer software that they, the parents, don't. In such cases the children's requests are likely to get more serious consideration from parents who want their children to have anything that will contribute to their success in life. "No sacrifice is too great to give my child all the things I didn't have in order to insure her happiness," is how one caring mother said it, and she probably summarizes the motives of Chinese mothers in general for ceding so much household decision making to their children (McNeal and Wu, 1995).

❏ *Children's personal expenditures*

Plate 2 was drawn by a nine-year-old who was asked to "draw what comes to your mind when you think about going shopping." The youngster's drawing shows him stepping boldly up to the toy counter of a department store with a five-yuan note in his hand. It's his money, and he is attracted to the sign above the salesperson that reads, "Ship models on sale." And the sign to his right beckons him with, "Welcome. Visit our store." What this youngster is saying in his drawing is that he has money to spend and he wants to spend it, in this case on play items.

Chinese children's economic clout is mainly due to their enormous influence on their parents' purchases that was discussed above. But there is another element that is very important to many marketers and advertisers — that of the children's spending of their own money on their own wants and needs — that is demonstrated in this drawing. Like Western children, children in China's big cities have money to spend and spend it, with and without parents' assistance. Where do they get the money? From mom and dad, of course, and chances are some from grandparents and other relatives. In a study conducted among almost 1,500 families in urban China, parents reported that their children have money to spend by age 4 — and start spending it then in many cases (McNeal and Yeh, 1997). The children's income consists of two equally important types, according to the study. One is money that is given frequently to children for spending that the researchers term, *regular income.* They found three main sources of regular income. The primary source, accounting for 40 percent, consists of frequent small gifts of money from parents. This money is usually given to children of all ages on an as-needed basis, and the amount tends to be related somewhat to the number of requests made by the children. An allowance — what is described as a periodic distribution of money to children with usually no specific conditions attached — constitutes the second most important source of regular income and averages 32 percent. Children from age four on may receive an allowance, but it is more likely to be given to children ages eight and above. Money gifts from other, mainly grandparents who live in the children's homes, make up 22 percent of their regular income. Finally, three percent of regular income, mainly for 11- and 12-year-olds comes from work in the home — usually cleaning and repairing — and a similar amount, again mainly for the older children, comes from work outside the home such as selling food goods in the streets. The researchers also reported that the children receive what they call *special income* that is given to the children by parents and grandparents during special occasions; namely, Chinese New Year, Children's Day, Moon Festival, and on birthdays. Red packet money, call *hong bau,* that is given during the two weeks of celebrating the Lunar New Year, is by far the largest money gift, and 60 percent of parents indicate in the research that the money is expected to be saved. Thus, Chinese children not only have money to spend, but money to save.

Table 1-3 reveals that the average weekly income — including

Table 1-3: **Mean weekly income, spending, saving of urban Chinese children by age**

Age	Income (yuan)	Spending (yuan)	Saving (yuan)/Rate (%)
4	3.2	0.8	2.4 (75)
5	4.8	1.4	3.4 (71)
6	6.5	2.2	4.3 (66)
7	8.2	3.1	5.1 (62)
8	12.0	5.3	7.7 (64)
9	14.5	5.5	9.0 (62)
10	16.3	6.1	10.2 (63)
11	18.4	7.8	10.6 (57)
12	21.1	10.3	10.8 (51)

regular and special income — increases significantly with age of children and ranges from 3.2 yuan for four-year-olds to 21.1 yuan for 12-year-olds. The table somewhat disguises the large lumps of special income by averaging all income on a weekly basis. Actually, around 70 percent of income of four-year-olds consists of special income; for 12-year-olds it is roughly 50 percent. While all children receive some special income, not all have regular income. Only 21 percent of 4s, 28 percent of 5s, 34 percent of 6s, 49 percent of 7s, and 77 percent of 8s have some regular income, while all those ages 9 and above have some regular income.

The children in this study average spending around 40 percent of their total income. Table 1-3 shows that there is very little spending among the 4s and 5s, typically around one yuan per week. Once the children reach age 8, however, they spend at least five yuan per week, and that doubles by age 12. So, both income and spending increase age-step. Boys spend more than girls apparently because the older boys are allowed to take some of their savings out of the bank and spend it.

Researchers asked the parents to what extent their children go to the marketplace with them, as well as on their own, in order to make purchases. They reported that most of their children of all ages make some independent purchases while shopping with them or the grandparents. The average number of shopping trips per week with parents during which children make purchases amounts to around two, with somewhat less being taken by the very young and the older children.

On their own, the children ages 8 and above make two or three purchase-visits a week. It should be noted that retailers and residences are located together in urban China, as compared to cities in the United States, for example, where zoning laws often separate the two. Thus, the children can easily get to some kind of shopping facilities. Also, most children walk to and from school and usually do some shopping and buying on these daily travels.

The number and kinds of stores visited by the children were examined in this study. Typically the children visit one store a week with parents and around two a week without them, or an average of slightly less than three a week. The most frequently visited type of store is a food store followed by book stores, toy stores and stationery stores. A few of the older children mentioned department stores as places to shop.

Parents were asked in the study to estimate how their children allocate their money to eight product categories that were determined in a pilot study: snacks, books and magazines, school supplies, play items (including pay-to-play video games), clothing, sporting goods, recorded music, and electronic items. The average results for all children are as follows: snacks, 21 percent, books and magazines, 31 percent, school supplies, 25 percent, clothing, 10 percent, play items, 8 percent, music, 2 percent, sporting goods, 2 percent, and electronics, 1 percent. Children, 4–8, allocate significantly more of their money to snacks and play items, while 9–12s allocate significantly more of their money to books, clothing and electronics. Thus, over half (31 plus 25 percent) of their own money is spent on educational items. There are no significant differences in the percentage of spending by boys and girls among the categories.

In total, the children in this study spent an average of US$1 per week, or slightly over US$50 a year. If we extend these figures to the 100 million children who live in urban China only, we can see that they spend at least US$5 billion a year on a relatively wide range of products in a relatively wide range of shopping settings. Today, however, we can expect the expenditure to be much greater than in this 1997 report as household incomes have grown rapidly. Also, the above study was conducted only among children 12 and under. Those in their early teens would likely spend much more per person.

Children in the study average *saving* about 60 percent of their income, according to Table 1-3. As noted, special income which constitutes a majority of children's income is expected to be saved and thus drives up the saving rate of the children. Of their regular income, children save about 30 percent. Most of the children's savings, according to this study, are kept in commercial depositories with only small amounts kept at home. It is important to emphasize here that Chinese children are given money to teach them the consumer behavior of saving as well as that of spending. To oversimplify somewhat, they are given money regularly to spend, and on special occasions such as Lunar New Year they are given substantial amounts that are expected to be saved. We must look beyond China's historically socialist economy to its culture to understand the strong emphasis on saving money. The early saving of money in Chinese childhood contributes to the development of one's prestige, or face, or what the Chinese would call *mian zi*. Saving is also a way of learning to balance one's life, of not giving in entirely to one's impulses to splurge, or what Confucius termed "the mean" (Yau, 1988). So saving, like spending, satisfies several important needs. It permits planned spending, particularly for relatively expensive items such as computers and computer software, and it enhances one's dignity and one's feelings of security and contentment. In Western nations commercial banks target kids with advertising and marketing in order to attract them to open savings accounts. With the substantial rate of savings for Chinese children, we can expect that banks will do the same in China.

❑ *Children as a future market*

As noted above, commercial banks may target children as current savers — to get them to open and maintain a savings account — but also target them as *future* depositors (McNeal, 1991). That is, by attracting children to a bank to establish a savings account, the children become attached to the bank and eventually (in the future), according to marketing theory as well as the hopes of the bank, they will open a checking account, obtain a credit card from the bank, and even open a business account. In effect, the bank is targeting the children as current customers — savers — and as future customers. Increasing numbers of businesses are recognizing that there are only two sources of new customers. Either they are obtained from competitors or they are developed from childhood. The normal business model is a competitive one and suggests that new customers can be obtained from competitors. So, they vie for customers with attention-getting efforts such as advertising and promotions. But those same businesses may "grow" customers from childhood, that is, attract children's attention to the business, its product offering, and its brands. This is what McDonald's does, for example. It has a part of its marketing program targeting youth — from the time they are infants to the time they are grown. It has Kids Meals, it has play areas, it offers birthday parties and promotional items, and it uses Ronald McDonald to "talk" to the kids. It also targets kids with advertising and publicity both in media and in schools. All the time, of course, it is also targeting parents and adults.

The idea behind targeting children as future consumers is to provide a steady stream of new customers when they reach market age for a particular firm. By nurturing them as future customers, the kids become comfortable with the brand name, the manufacturer or store offering, and the prices of the offering. So to speak, they become a customer at a very early age, although they may not buy anything until they are teens or young adults.

If a business such as a bank or a department store can attract the children to the place of business and get the children to spend some money, or get the children to bring their parents to spend their money, then a relationship can be formed with the children. And the children will grow into regular customers for the business. Thus, advertising — the major topic of this book — can be one major tool that is used to maintain the relationship, to keep a channel of communications open to the children. That is the practice of McDonald's and Kentucky Fried Chicken in China, for example, but in Western countries this is also common marketing strategy among airlines, clothing retailers, and nonprofit organizations such as museums and zoos, to name a few (McNeal, 1992).

❑ *When do children become consumers?*

We established that Chinese children are consumers by spending their own money and directing the spending of much of their parents' money. When does all this begin? Children are not born as consumers, although they appear to be born to shop. The research that produced the data on children's spending and influence on parents' spending gives some clues about the time table of becoming a consumer. Let us look at this briefly from the standpoint of a five-stage model used to describe consumer behavior development in the United States (McNeal, 1993). It should be noted that these stages are based mainly on behavior and are not cognitive stages, although they are related just as all behavior and thinking are related.

❏ *Stage one: Observing*

Most of an infant's waking hours are spent trying to understand his/her world. Thus, their untrained senses that they are born with — seeing, hearing, touching, tasting, and smelling — get a real workout early in life. One of their applications is in the marketplace. Chinese mothers (and grandmothers) take children to the marketplace — to stores, street kiosks, night markets — often by necessity, but it is from these visits that the children first learn about it. Somewhere during the first six-months of life the children began experiencing the sights, sounds, and smells of the marketplace. Since their minds are essentially "empty slates," they absorb much of these experiences in the form of impressions. Along with the visits mom may provide her baby with some special treats, for example, a taste of ice cream. Pairing the store visit with a treat reinforces the baby's impressions of the marketplace as a positive object or place. Thus, in the very early months of life children become aware of the marketplace and probably associate it with positive thoughts.

❏ *Stage two: Requesting*

After many visits to the marketplace and after providing the children with all of his/her needs and wants, mom and the children communicate well about their likes and dislikes. At some point, probably around twenty-four months, the child begins to make requests for certain items when they are seen in the marketplace. Usually what occurs is that pleasurable products that children receive at home are seen in the store, a connection is made, and the child asks for them with words and gestures. At this point the child begins to realize that those sweets and play items provided by parents and grandparents can be found in the marketplace. Requests are likely to increase from this point on as mom obtains much pleasure from satisfying her child's wants and needs that are expressed through requests. At this point, also, some marketers view the child as a member of the influence market, and try to get their sales messages to the child via the mother, in-store displays, and advertising on television. Thus, at around two-years-old marketing messages about products-that-teach, sweet and salty snacks, and play items begin to search out the child. What we see at around two-years-old is the toddler's consumer behavior emerging and marketing activities responding accordingly.

❏ *Stage three: Selecting*

In the United States most goods are sold in self-service settings, and at around three-and-a-half-years-old children begin to select products from store shelves. This occurs at a time when the child has developed his or her motor skills and can accomplish this feat. In China there is much less self-service — although it is growing rapidly to assist the time-starved parents — and selection is less common. But in the street markets, the new supermarkets, and in toy, clothing, and food departments of department stores, children do begin to assert their developed walking and reaching, and by all means their memories that catalog the locations of desirable goods and services. Again, this physical consumer behavior occurs at around three or four years old and is a precursor to making purchases.

❏ *Stage four: Co-purchasing*

At around age four to five, some Chinese children begin to ask mom to let them buy things. Noticeably, they have money, often obtained as gifts from grandparents and others, including the parents, and have observed one of its main purposes — to be exchanged for goods and services. Seeing mom and dad and other shoppers buy things with money, the child begins to reason that she or he can do the same thing. At some time before the children enter the first-grade, they may attempt to make a purchase with the assistance of their parents. This co-purchasing is likely to continue for a year or so until the youngsters have practiced it enough to perform independently. Also, in addition to their help, the parents must give permission to the children to make purchases, at least initially. But at this point, usually before the entry to elementary school, the child is beginning to look like a customer to some retailers and producers.

❏ *Stage five: Independent purchasing*

Following many experiences at parental assisted purchases, the final step in becoming a consumer occurs: the solo purchase. Between ages six to eight the child is likely to be permitted to attempt a purchase, usually at a neighborhood store or street kiosk. There usually is a significant time period between a child's first purchase with parents and a completely independent purchase. During this interval children gain a better understanding of money and the exchange process, and they mature enough, physically and mentally, to persuade parents that they are capable of making a purchase on their own. Chances are the purchase will be a food or beverage, but it will rapidly become more complex such as school supplies at a convenience store while walking to school. At this point, the child is considered a bona fide consumer by marketers and a legitimate target for marketing messages — as a primary market and influence market.

❏ *Why do children buy*

It is apparent, then, that Chinese children rapidly grow into consumers, and by elementary school time are making some purchases on their own, with and without the help of parents. And, on a larger scale, these children are asking parents and grandparents to buy for them a wider variety of products and services. An important question arises: What motivates Chinese children to want and buy products? There appears to be no research that has focused primarily on Chinese children's buying motives, but from studies of what they buy and what they request parents to buy for them, these reasons can be deduced, at least to a descriptive extent.

When Chinese children's consumer behavior is examined, there appears to be four basic explanations for it, or we might term *predominant needs* (McNeal, 1992). (We are using the psychological model that assumes that unmet needs motivate children to obtain products and services that will satisfy these needs.) These predominant needs are encapsulated in the following statements Chinese children have made in research programs (in no particular order).

1. "To have fun:" This statement and similar statements — "To play," "To have fun with friends," — indicate that *play*, as the psychologist Henry Murray calls it, is important to Chinese children just as it is to children around the world. For most children play often takes priority over eating and sleeping. For example, they may not want to stop playing in order to eat or go to bed. It should be noted that Chinese parents like to limit the amount of play that their children perform, and prefer to see the children spend more of their time with studies. This may be the first serious parent-child conflict since play is theorized to be essential. Therefore, products that provide a combination of play and education — that satisfy the motives of both child and parents — may be more successful than those that offer only fun.

2. "To be with friends:" As children discover others — parents, peers, pets — they want to be with them. Psychologists call this the need for *affiliation*, that is, the need to have cooperative relations with others. This does not appear to be a need specific to a collective society such as China, but like play, seems to be universal. It is implied by statements such as, "I like to play with friends," "I want to be with my classmates," "I like to go shopping with my mother." In fact, children often elect to be with their peers, rather than their parents, in such activities as playing and shopping. Consequently, marketers that offer children products that are to be shared, that "lets you have fun together," are likely to be appealing to children, at least those of school age.

3. "I like the taste of McDonald's:" Young children seem to be testing their newly developed sensory system by tasting new

flavors such as those that might be found at a Western restaurant. But they also show a desire to express other senses such as touching, smelling, hearing, and seeing. Murray, the psychologist, calls this the need for *sentience*, although it sometimes is seen as the discovery need, or the need for new experiences. Infants can be observed rubbing the material of mother's blouse between their fingers, seemingly just to touch, to feel. Thus, it is likely that products that emphasize, for example, new flavors, new colors, different sounds will particularly appeal to the younger children.

4. "I want to make good grades:" Chinese children, more than Western children, for example, seem to consider accomplishments as very important. Thus, comments like, "I like to go to English class after school" and "I want to be on the volleyball team" suggest that *achievement*, as the psychologist might term it, is a significant need to Chinese children, perhaps even more than for Western children. So, products that promise more strength, better grades, more friends, more fun, are likely to be attractive to school-age kids.

It is concluded by motivational psychologists that all people possess the same needs — both children and adults — but that they prioritize them differently. For example, a brief observation of adults in daily activities would show that the play need is not very important, while the opposite is likely to be the case for kids. So, there are a number of other needs that we might suggest as being important to children in addition to the four noted above. But these four needs — play, affiliation, sentience, and achievement — stand out in research as being predominant in the behavioral patterns of kids. Look again at Plate 1. The children were asked to draw what they think of when they think of the long weekend. The child who drew this picture pretty well summarizes his important needs, and they seem to be these four needs noted above. Obviously playing is significant — it takes center stage. Sentience shows up with the McDonald's sign and destination. Affiliation is clear as the illustrator includes his friends in his activities. And achievement, while less apparent, is suggested by the athletic clothing. It does not seem like a far stretch to expect marketers who successfully target kids in China to offer the satisfaction of these needs, and to offer most or all four in specific products and services.

Conclusions

So, why do advertisers target Chinese children? Because they are a market? Yes, but actually because they are not one market but *three* markets in one. They are a *primary* market, spending their own money on their own wants and needs, they are an *influence* market that determines much of the spending of their parents, and they are a *future* market for *all* goods and services who have all their purchases ahead of them. Theoretically, then, children are three markets in one person, and as such, have more market potential than any other demographic group. That's why advertisers target kids, and why we will devote the remainder of this book to saying this in detail.

Perhaps the nine-year-old child who drew Plate 3 says it best. When asked to "draw what comes to your mind when you think about going shopping," he drew children in a Beijing department store performing as members of all three markets. He is racing to the toy counter with money in hand to buy a play item — a primary market. Another youngster is doing the same thing at the clothing counter (under the sign that says, "Welcome, hello, customers.") Yet, another child (in the middle of the drawing) has mom in tow, co-shopping with her — an influence market. Finally, another child is shopping in the appliance department under the sign that states that appliances are on sale. This child apparently envisions a later time when he will be providing for a household — a future market. Thus, a picture really is "worth a thousand words" as well as the hundreds of pages that we will devote to our topic of advertising to children.

❏ *Layout of the book*

In the next chapter, Chapter 2, we will put advertising in children's perspective by talking about their interactions with advertising media. Specifically, with research we will show where Chinese children obtain information about the products that they buy and ask their parents and grandparents to buy. Of course, advertising is one of these major sources of information.

In Chapter 3, we will look at children's understanding of television advertising. Does their understanding vary by age, sex, level of television viewing and level of advertising development? We will answer this question.

In Chapter 4, we are going to see whether Chinese children believe in television commercials. Does trust vary by age, sex, and level of advertising development? How do they know which commercials are true and which are not? Do they trust in advertised brands, when compared with non-advertised brands? Thorough answers to these questions will be provided.

In Chapter 5, we are going to see whether children watch television commercials when they are on, and whether they like television commercials. And we will answer the question, "Do attitudes toward television advertising vary by age, sex and level of advertising development?"

In Chapter 6, we examine how parents communicate with children about consumption, and how parent-child communication patterns vary by demographics of parents and different dynamic relationships.

In Chapter 7, we investigate what parents think about television advertising in general, and advertising towards children in specific. We also report how Chinese parents exert control over children's viewing of television. Also, we will show how parents' attitudes toward advertising correlate with their children's attitudes toward advertising.

In Chapter 8, we devote our attention to the advertisements themselves. Using a content analysis technique, we examine what are the advertising appeals and cultural values employed in the television commercials targeted at children in China. We also compare children's commercials in China with their counterparts in the United States.

In Chapter 9, we review the rules and regulations governing children's advertising in China. We will introduce the existing ordinance and examine how it is interpreted. We discuss the censorship system, the regulation and self-regulation of advertising in China. We also discuss advertising executions that are found to be acceptable or violating the advertising regulations.

Finally, in Chapter 10, we pull together the essentials of the research findings using two summary tables, draw some conclusions from them, and make some suggestions about how the information can be used by advertisers, parents, various social groups and the public policy makers.

Throughout the book, our emphasis is on television advertising. This is because television plays the most important role in children's consumer socialization. In the western societies, over 90 percent of the advertising dollars target at children go to the television (McNeal, 1992). We suppose the case for China will be pretty much the same, too.

Chapter 2

Role of Mass Media in the Consumer Socialization of Chinese Children: Putting Advertising in Focus

In Chapter 1 it was established that Chinese children make purchases as well as ask their parents to make purchases for them. In combination the children constitute a significant market that obtains and consumes a wide range of products. How do Chinese children learn about all of these products? Specifically, how do they learn of the products' existence, their functions, the needs they satisfy, how to utilize them, where to buy them? There are many possible sources of information for the children to process, both commercial and non-commercial. In this chapter we give consideration to all these sources with particular concern for advertising media.

The process of learning about products, their brands, and the retail outlets where they can be bought is called consumer socialization (Ward, 1974). Theory says that children learn consumer behavior patterns from parents first and foremost, but also from other socialization agents; namely, peers, schools, stores, media, and the products themselves and their packages (Moschis, 1987). Media's influence on children is mainly due to two dimensions — advertising and editorial/programming content (O'Guinn and Shrum, 1997) — with advertising specifically intended to inform young consumers about products and encourage their purchase. Advertising, as the term is used here, mainly refers to marketing messages presented by an identified sponsor in mass media such as the internet, magazines, newspapers, radio and television. The term may also be used to refer to point-of-purchase communications, that is, message presentation in the marketplace, in and around stores including outdoor signs and indoor signs. The term may also be extended to include product placement, that is, showing a product in use within a television program or movie to which the target audience will be exposed.

For advertising to be effective, the media must reach the children, or said another way, the children must reach the media since they interact with the media of their choice. But does this happen in developing China? If so, to what extent? And to what extent do Chinese children utilize advertising media in their quest for information about products? These questions have long been answered in Western nations such as Canada, United States, and Europe. But what about China, where the largest population of children can be found? We will attempt to shed light on these questions by examining some key research that has been conducted among Chinese children and their parents, research that examines the sources of product information utilized by children including the major media.

Interpersonal sources of product information

There are two principal interpersonal sources from which children learn about products and their consumption: parents and peers.

❏ *Parents as consumer socialization agents*

It has been shown for years in Western nations that the parents are probably most instrumental in teaching young people basic rational aspects of consumption such as satisfying many of their needs in the marketplace, understanding price-quality relationships, handling money wisely, and obtaining appropriate information before making purchases (e.g. McNeal, 1987; Ward et. al., 1977). Evidence suggests that the more often that parents or other caretakers take children shopping, the more conscious the children become of information about products such as their brands and prices (Shim et. al., 1995). Family communications may influence a child's interaction with other socialization agents, such as mass media and peer groups, which may also influence consumer learning. Moreover, there is considerable evidence to suggest that family communication processes modify the effects of other socialization agents (McLeod et. al., 1982) in particular the medium of television, and this parental mediation is often the result of a child's requests for advertised products (Atkin, 1982). In China the parents are known to be the paramount source of influence on their children, and are generally reputed to control the children's reliance on other information sources (Yau, 1988).

❏ *Peers as consumer socialization agents*

Like parents, peers can directly and indirectly affect children's consumer socialization. Several studies suggest that children learn the symbolic meaning of goods or expressive elements of consumption from their peers at school and at play (Moschis and Churchill, 1978; Moschis and Moore, 1982). For example, they learn from their friends what clothing styles are in fashion and when they go out of fashion. In addition, peers play an important role in the development of children's preference for stores, products, brands of selected products, media, and television programs. It is theoretically and empirically known that if child A likes child B, and if child B likes a brand of product, then child A will also like that brand. There is increasing evidence, also, that materialism and susceptibility to peer influence are positively related, suggesting that the more that children let peers influence them, the more products the children want and buy. In China the prevalence of the single-child household would seem to give even more than normal regard to peers as playmates, school chums, and confidants, and therefore, as influencers of children's consumer behavior patterns.

Commercial sources of product information

There are a number of commercial sources of information about products and their attributes, but two — media and retailers — have been empirically shown to be particularly important.

❏ *Retailers as consumer socialization agents*

Retailers logically can be expected to be significant sources of information about products. They stock the products, they display them, they advertise them in the stores and in media, they demonstrate them in the stores, and they interact frequently with children as customers. For instance, as was mentioned in Chapter 1, most Chinese children accompany their parents to the marketplace and make some purchases for themselves (McNeal and Yeh, 1997). Further, some of the children as young as four or five go to the marketplace on their own, and practically all of them beyond age eight venture into the marketplace alone to buy things. In total, the children make an average of three or four visits a week to retail outlets. Therefore, they are likely to receive much information from retailers via displays, packaging, point-of-purchase materials and from the store clerks since most Chinese retailing is still full-service rather than self-service — the goods are behind the counter, inside the counter, and available only through the clerks. Retailers also contribute to children's formation of attitudes, values, and behavioral patterns, including in-store shopping patterns, through various policies and operation procedures. In China's cities there is more neighborhood retailing than there is in most Western cities where zoning laws may forbid it. Therefore, going to retail outlets — stores and street kiosks — is convenient for children who may find shopping literally outside their apartment. In these cases, it seems that the retailers would be a very important source of product information.

❏ *Media as consumer socialization agents*

Advertising media, the major focus of this chapter, have probably received more attention in the research literature than any other consumer socialization agent (See Moschis, 1987 for a review). Both advertising and editorial/program content of the mass media provide children with knowledge and guidance in their consumer behavior development. In fact, it is often difficult to separate the influence, for example, of television advertising and television programming. It is made even more difficult by the fact that sometimes the spokesperson or spokescharacter in the advertisement is also a member of the program. Moreover, brands that are advertised in magazines or on TV for children may also be mentioned in the editorial content of magazines and radio and shown in use in television programming (Russell, 2002). Another factor that makes media important as influencers is their ubiquity. They are everywhere — in the home, in the child's room, at school, on the computer, on the way to school, in the car, on the bus. It is generally believed by the business world that what is prominent in the media becomes salient in the minds of the public, and in turn produces consumer-related behaviors such as shopping and purchasing (Sutherland and Galloway, 1981). This thinking is particularly important in the case of children where it is believed that many of the consumer attitudes and behavior they develop will be applied throughout much of their lives (Guest, 1955). Thus, since they have all of their purchases ahead of them, the impact of media advertising on children can be even greater than that on adults.

The influence of mass media advertising on children may indirectly be felt by their parents. In fact, marketers may plan it this way. Children who receive messages from the media may in turn convey these messages to their parents, perhaps in the form of requests for products. This two-step flow of influence on the gatekeeper has been practiced at least since the advent of television, that is, the message is directed to children who in turn direct it to parents (McNeal, 1999). Coming from the children generally gives the commercial message much more persuasive power and credibility than if it came directly from the advertiser. Advertisers have perfected this tactic to the point that they are frequently accused by parents of turning children into naggers.

Finally, the amount of interaction with the media appears to be positively related to learning consumer behavior. That is, the more that children interact with the mass media, the more consumer socialization takes place (Moschis and Churchill, 1978). Consequently, media advertise themselves to children in order to attract the children to the media more frequently. The net result is that children watch a particular television program regularly or read a particular magazine regularly. And the more viewers and readers, the more that advertisers pay the particular media.

Media in China

China's rapid change to a market-driven economy from one that is state-controlled is producing an average annual economic grow rate of around eight percent, far greater than that of any other large nation. And this is happening in a country that is still at least two-thirds rural. It is China's urban areas that are producing most of its economic growth. For example, its ten largest cities contain only 4 percent of its population but account for approximately 22 percent of earning power and 19 percent of discretionary spending. Consequently, a major growth in media has occurred as a direct response to this growth in consumer spending. New media, changing media, growing media are logical reactions to higher personal and household incomes. (And we should keep in mind that rising incomes are usually tied to rising educational levels in a population that also stimulates the development of new and improved media.) New media, such as new magazines and newspapers, not only provide outlets for advertising, but also provide satisfaction to those members of the population, such as children, that are seeking information and entertainment.

The fast development of television broadcasting has been most notable. Television now reaches over 92 percent of China's households through almost 400 broadcasting stations, in spite of many areas still being impoverished (Bu, 2001). For instance, in 1995 there were 114 color TVs per 100 households in Beijing compared with only 36 in 1987. Moreover, in 1999 there were eight national channels and 53 local channels broadcasting around ten hours of programs per day for children compared to only three channels 15 years earlier and virtually no specific programs for children (Bu, 2001). Today, a typical TV schedule of the national television channel, China Central Television (CCTV) in January 2003 (see Appendix 2-1) shows that the content of programming that targets children consists of one to two hours of cartoon entertainment in the morning for preschoolers such as *Cartoon City*, and one to two hours of entertainment after school. The remaining hours when children might view television, with their parents or alone, tend to have an educational slant such as teaching values, English, singing, and other school topics. On average the national channels carry about 9.5 hours of children's programs and the local channels carry about 0.5 hour of children's programs every day. Children's preference for television programs change with age. Younger audience like to watch cartoons, children's drama series, games shows and variety shows. Teenagers become more interested in sports programs and news programs (Bu, 1998).

As for other major media, in 1995 there were around 115 radios per 100 Chinese households. In 1999, there were 299 radio stations that reached over 90 percent of China's households mainly targeting adults, usually with news, economic matters, and music, but there was some after-school programming of one hour or less that targets children with both education and entertainment. Popular children's programs include *Small Trumpet* for young children ages 5–7, *Fire Pole* and *Rainbow Bridge* for elementary school children, and *439 Station* for secondary school children (Bu, 2001).

Similar growth in other new media has also occurred, and today there are 2,235 newspapers in China with Beijing having 240. And there are more than 8,000 magazines now published in China with 1,884 available in Beijing. Owing to China's lack of a good national distribution system, most of the print media are of a local or regional nature. In 1997 there were 77 newspapers and 98 magazines targeting children (Bu, 2001) with virtually all of them tending toward the educational, and with very little that children would be likely to perceive as fun for fun's sake. One tabloid that is popular with Chinese children in virtually all of the major cities of China is *Zhong guo shao nian bao* (Chinese children's news). It has been published since 1951 and its national circulation in 1997 was 0.9 million (Bu, 2001). It presents stories about heroes and heroines who are revered by children and their parents in order to teach values and love for the nation.

The commercial content among print media that target children can generally be described as sparse. In 1998 there were one or two advertisements, at most, per children's magazine or newspaper, and they were usually targeted at parents and typically focused on health and/or educational products. For example, in an issue of *The King of Story* there was a full page ad for Signal toothbrushes that targeted both parents and children with a health message. Advertisements tend to be more prevalent in broadcast media — which we will talk about in detail in later chapters. There is usually a 15-second commercial before and after each radio program and each television program that targets children. These ads are directed at parents and children, and those to children in around 88 percent of cases, present messages about foods and beverages such as *Wahaha*, a Chinese soft drink, while the remainder consists of messages about school supplies, video games, and toiletries such as Little White Rabbit toothpaste. Advertisements from Western marketers that target children are beginning to appear, but still constitute only a small portion of the money spent by advertisers to reach children. For example, in the content analysis of Beijing television commercials that target children that is described in Chapter 8, only ten of several hundred ads were for Western products including McDonald's, KFC, and Oreo cookies.

Table 2-1 displays the production of media goods for Chinese children and youth in 1996 and 2001. It shows that new media such as video compact disks, laser video disks and compact disks enjoy a much higher growth rate than traditional media such as books. It also indicates for a vast country with 300 million children, the production of children's media goods have much room for development.

Chinese children's media habits

Studies of media usage in China, especially among its children, appear to be uncommon and certainly not comprehensive. However, we would expect that the children's media habits would reflect those of their parents. For example, in a 1995 study of media habits by Gallup China Ltd., 86 percent of urban adults said they had watched television, around 50

Table 2-1: **Production of media goods for children**

Media	1996		2001		Average annual % change	
	No. of titles	Volume	No. of titles	Volume	No. of titles	Volume
Books (exclude textbooks)	3,053	143,870,000	7,254	228,750,000	19%	10%
Audio cassette tapes	752	8,418,600	847	7,576,000	2%	−2%
Compact disks (CDs)	70	98,600	136	802,400	14%	52%
Video tapes	165	336,300	14	49,100	−39%	−32%
Video compact disks (VCDs)	44	177,000	708	8,432,800	74%	117%
Laser video disks	12	8,000	29	337,000	19%	111%

Sources: Bu, 2001; China Audio Visual and Film Net, 2002.

percent had listened to radio, 74 percent of urban dwellers had read a newspaper, and 54 percent had read a magazine (Li and Gallup, 1995). While the survey did not include children, it does suggest that China's kids will be familiar with all the media and have some experience with them. To the extent that children are heavy media users, it follows that they rely on the media for information about new products of interest to them.

In a survey of 2,288 Beijing children in 1998, the most popular media were television, books and newspapers (Bu, 1998). The media exposure in a week was: watching television (89 percent), reading books (73 percent), reading newspapers (73 percent), listening to cassette tapes (65 percent), listening to radio (61 percent), reading magazines (53 percent), playing with computers (32 percent), playing electronic games (14 percent) and surfing on the internet (7 percent).

With this background we examine what appears to be the first study to determine where Chinese children as consumers obtain information about new products and their attitudes toward different sources of information (McNeal and Ji, 1999).

❏ *How the research was done*

Since the investigators wanted to know what sources of information, including media, the children employed to find out about new products, some fundamental research procedures were utilized. The children were provided with a list of products and asked where they learned about each. Additionally, children's perceptions of the relative importance of different information sources were examined by asking them to rank sources from a list given to them. Both the list of the products and the list of information sources were identified in a pilot study conducted a few weeks earlier among 58 Beijing children in grades 4–6. From the pilot study it was found that mass media played an unexpectedly important role in providing new product information for Chinese children. Consequently, it was decided to administer a separate questionnaire to parents in order to learn about mass media usage by their children.

The final study design was conducted among 460 children in grades

4, 5, and 6 in three elementary schools, one each from the North, East, and West of the Beijing metropolitan area. The specific schools were selected by Beijing elementary school officials to be representative of children in grades 4–6 in the Beijing area as a whole. The boys and girls in these grades ranged in age from eight to 13 years, and were chosen because they were expected to be mature enough to sort objects such as media and evaluate them. Children were grouped into youngest (8–9), middle (10–11), and oldest (12–13) for convenience of analysis, recognizing that within the age range of eight to 13 years, children's information processing abilities such as reading and listening may vary with age.

The two questionnaires that were utilized in this study were first constructed in English and then translated into Chinese, tested, modified, and tested again. The children were administered one questionnaire at school regarding their new product information sources. They were also asked to take the other questionnaire about their media usage habits home to their parents for completion and return it to their teachers within three days. A small gift was promised to the children to encourage the return of it. A net total of 409 children and their corresponding families completed the questionnaires with 47.7 percent from girls and 52.3 percent from boys. All questionnaires sent to parents were completed by mothers who in 98.9 percent of cases had only one child. In addition, the questionnaires revealed that all household in this study owned at least one television set and one radio, 90.7 percent subscribed to or bought one newspaper for their children to read, and 70.4 percent subscribed to or bought at least one children's magazine.

As noted, a list of 17 products was provided and the children were asked to report what was the most likely source for them to learn about a new type of each. They were asked to write the name of the source in a blank adjacent to each product. In all, the children mentioned 20 different sources and each was assigned to one of nine general categories of sources previously determined in the pilot study. For these nine categories of information sources the children also were asked to rank the three most important ones (with a 1, 2, 3) from which they learned about new products. (This question was positioned in the questionnaire so that it would minimize any effect on the children's responses to the questions in the previous part.) The children were asked for information sources for any new products, rather than for specific products such as toys and snacks, in order to cue the children's attitudes toward sources in general rather than just toward media and media advertising.

A second questionnaire regarding children's media usage habits, which was coded to correspond to each child who completed a questionnaire, was taken home to parents. The first part asked for some demographics of the household. The next part consisted of four three-part questions about their children's media use — do they watch TV, listen to the radio, read newspapers and magazines, and if so, what kinds of programs/materials do they regularly watch/listen to/read, and how much time do they devote to each medium each weekday and weekend day? Since it is almost impossible for either children or their parents to report the extent of their children's usage of outdoor advertising, the study did not attempt to obtain data about it in this part of the study.

Data were examined mainly according to age as is typically done in consumer socialization studies of children. The chi-square test of independence was used to explore the differences among age groups. The findings were also examined for effects of gender and family occupation. The chi-square test of independence was also utilized to investigate the relationship between the types of product information sources and the types of products. Principle factor analysis and varimax rotation methods were used to classify the 17 products into groups.

Children's relative use of information sources

Results of the research show that the sources that children use to learn about new products are highly related to types of products. The 17 products that the children were asked about were factor analyzed into four groups (factors). These are listed in Table 2-2 along with their factor loadings. Relative use of nine information sources to find out about each of the four groups by Chinese children was calculated. These results are shown in Table 2-3. Considering the two tables together will define the importance of each information source.

Table 2-2: **Summary of rotated factor analysis of products according to children's information sources**

Factors	Factor loading
Factor 1 — School items	
Cassette players	0.69
Clothing	0.62
Shoes	0.59
Bicycles	0.46
Computers	0.45
Books	0.39
Factor 2 — Personal care items	
Toothpaste	0.70
Soap	0.67
Shampoo	0.59
Factor 3 — Snacks	
Gum	0.66
Candy	0.49
Ice cream	0.48
Soft drinks	0.44
Cookies	0.35
Factor 4 — Play items	
Sports equipment	0.55
Toys	0.41
Video games	0.34

Table 2-3: **Children's relative use of nine information sources for four product groups**

Groups (factors)	Parents	Grand-parents	Friends	TV	Radio	News-papers	Maga-zines	Out-door ads	Store visits
School items	34.3	1.5	10.5	16.5	2.5	3.8	2.4	5.3	23.3
Personal care items	35.9	0.8	1.0	32.5	2.2	2.6	1.6	9.6	13.9
Snacks	13.8	0.7	10.1	27.3	2.8	2.4	2.4	10.1	30.5
Play items	17.1	0.6	20.5	22.4	2.8	2.1	2.9	6.9	22.6

❏ *Product group 1 — School items*

The products classified in the first group are mainly school-related, relatively expensive items — books, computers, cassette players, bicycles, clothing and shoes. The books, computers and cassette players are mainly learning aids, bicycles are transportation to and from school, and their clothing and shoes are primarily school wear. Not unexpected, parents play the most important role in the children's learning about new products in this group as shown in Table 2-3. Just over 34 percent listed parents as a source followed by 23.3 percent for stores and 16.5 per cent for TV. Gender has some effect with boys more than girls learning about shoes and computers from TV, perhaps to be sure of what is current in both.

❏ *Product group 2 — Personal care items*

This category includes soap, shampoo, and toothpaste, and parents and TV play an almost equal role in providing children with information about them — a total of 68.4 percent of children listed either of them. Ordinarily in China children use the personal care products used by their parents, so they look to parents for guidance. But it appears that TV is a growing source of information about these items as children seek out information about products just for them. And this seems to be the case for both boys and girls.

❏ *Product group 3 — Snacks*

The third group, consisting of gum, candy, ice cream, soft drinks and cookies, were classified as snacks. When learning about snacks it seems to be more important for children to look at the products themselves in stores (30.5 percent), on TV (27.3 percent), than to parents and friends. Thus, for these items Chinese children rely on commercial information sources three-quarters of the time. Perhaps this is by default since Chinese parents who perceive food almost solely from a health standpoint are unlikely to even suggest snack foods to their children.

❏ *Product group 4 — Play items*

The products in Group 4 are all play items — sports equipment, toys, and video games. On average, store visits (22.6 percent), TV (22.4 percent), and friends (20.5 percent) play an almost equal role as information sources, with parents being only slightly important (17.1 percent). Probably the number of nearly equal sources for play items reflects the importance of play to kids that motivates them to be alert to virtually any related information.

❏ *Summary of children's use of selected information sources*

In all, Table 2-3 shows that the percentage of children who utilize interpersonal sources — friends, parents, grandparents — to learn about new products are as follows: 46.3 percent for school-related, relatively expensive items; 37.7 percent for personal care items; 24.6 percent for snacks; and 38.2 percent for play items. The residuals are for commercial sources. Thus, somewhat contrary to previous research and caveats about strong reliance on others for guidance, this study reveals that Chinese children depend on commercial sources at least as much as they do on interpersonal sources to learn about new products. Or, observed from another direction, in no case do all interpersonal sources together provide at least 50 percent of information about new products to Beijing's kids.

Children's relative importance of new product information sources

In order to determine children's perceptions of product information sources, they were asked to rank their three most important sources of information about products new to them from a list of nine. These are listed in Table 2-4. Total rankings are the highest for television, 77.0 percent, with parents following a distant second with 47.7 percent. Store visits are third with 41.3 percent, friends next with 39.6 percent, with newspapers, radio, outdoor ads, magazines, and grandparents following in this order. When these sources are grouped into mass media, interpersonal, and stores, mass media win hands down with 668 mentions, followed by interpersonal with 390, and then stores with 169. So, Chinese children consider the mass media as the most important new product information source due mainly to the heavy influence of the relatively new medium of television.

Table 2-4: Ranking of new product information sources used by
Chinese children

Sources of information	First most important	Second most important	Third most important	Total rankings of each number (percent)
Television	197	61	57	315 (77.0%)
Parents	83	65	47	195 (47.7%)
Store visits	23	69	77	169 (41.3%)
Friends	28	55	79	162 (39.6%)
Newspapers	39	56	43	138 (33.8%)
Radio	18	43	42	103 (25.2%)
Outdoor ads	4	28	26	58 (14.2%)
Magazines	8	16	30	54 (12.2%)
Grandparents	9	16	8	33 (8.1%)
Total	409	409	409	1,227

From the standpoint of age, the importance of television as a new product information source increases significantly as children get older, while that of the other media remain fairly constant at their lower levels. Gender-wise, magazines are more important to boys than girls. Children whose parents are blue-collar workers are more likely to rank newspapers as one of their three most important information sources as compared to children of white-collar workers.

The lesser role of interpersonal sources is surprising in view of the great importance of family in Chinese society. Further analysis by age of children reveals that friends are considered as more important as the children grow older, while grandparents lose most of their influence and that of the parents declines slightly. Thus, parents do appear to be regarded as a fairly constant new product information source for the kids. But parents are not viewed as more important than the media even when their influence is combined with other persons. And the wisdom of age, of grandparents, is practically ignored by the kids in this study.

Stores do not play as important a role as Westerners might expect, coming in third overall with less than six percent giving them first place rankings. And this is consistent across gender and age.

Perhaps this difference is due to self-service not being as common among any Chinese store types as it is in the West. Therefore, Chinese children can seldom reach and examine products on the shelves by themselves easily and comfortably even though they frequently visit stores by themselves. And they cannot easily express their sentience need to touch and feel.

This major piece of research also examined four mass media separately — TV, radio, newspapers, and magazines — in order to determine if involvement in a medium was related to perceiving the medium as an important new product information source. Table 2-5 shows the percentage of Chinese children who use each of the four media and the average total hours they devote to each per week, according to their parents.

From the table we can see that TV viewing (97.3 percent) is much more common than readership of newspapers (72.9 percent) and magazines (60.4 percent), and radio listening (38.9 percent). Moreover, the average time that Chinese children devote to watching TV (17.2 hours) each week is far greater than the total spent on reading newspapers (2.7 hours) and magazines (2.6 hours) and listening to the radio (6.3 hours). The average of 17.2 hours a week of TV viewing results from an average of 1.8 hours during weekdays and 4.2 hours on weekend days. There are some gender differences in the use of three of the four media. Boys watch significantly more TV than girls on weekends (4.8 hours versus 3.8 hours), and their readership of magazines is slightly higher than that of girls (64.5 percent versus 55.3 percent). However, girls' readership of newspapers is significantly higher than that of boys (77.7 percent versus 68.2 percent). Age and family occupation seems to have little or no effect on children's media usage.

Table 2-5: **Comparative media usage among Chinese children**

Media	Usage (percent)	Hours per week
Television	97.3	17.2
Radio	38.9	6.3
Newspapers	72.9	2.7
Magazines	60.4	2.6

An examination of the relationships among Chinese children's usage of the four mass media reveals that 38.9 percent of them who listen to the radio are more likely to read newspapers and magazines compared to those who do not listen to the radio. On the other hand, heavy TV viewers (defined as those who watch more than 20 hours a week) are less likely to read newspapers than moderate TV viewers (defined as those who watch 14–20 hours a week) and light TV viewers (defined as those who watch less than 14 hours a week).

In the case of TV, the more time children devote to watching it, the more important it is regarded as a new product information source — 86.2 percent of heavy viewers, 79.1 of moderate viewers, and 62.9 percent of light viewers. There is a tendency for heavy TV viewers (46.4 percent) to regard friends as one of their most important sources of information as compared to moderate (37.4 percent) and light viewers (32.6 percent). But this relationship is probably due to age intervention, that is, as children get older they tend to watch more TV and concurrently turn to friends as more important information sources.

In the case of the other media, there appears to be less enthusiasm for them to be regarded as new product information sources even when there is significant usage of them. For example, only a slightly higher percentage of radio listeners (28.9 percent) reported radio as one of their most important sources than those who do not listen to it. And those children who regularly read newspapers and magazines do not look on them as significantly more important sources of new product information than those who do not.

Summing up

The data reported in this chapter reveal, perhaps for the first time, the interpersonal and commercial sources from which Chinese children learn about the new products they buy or ask their parents to buy. Earlier research concluded that traditional Chinese families rely heavily on word of mouth to learn about new products and much less on mass media (Yau, 1994). This current study, however, shows that urban Chinese children tend to rely on commercial sources at least as much as they do on interpersonal sources to obtain new product information. This is in contrast to the Chinese's sheltered image and their strong family orientation. It has long been held that the Chinese have a very distinct and consistent value system which has endured for many generations that is based on the importance of interpersonal relationships in all decision making. Yet, the findings reported here demonstrate that a new consumer generation is emerging in China that is more exposed to and more open to commercial sources. As a result, they may be more heavily influenced by the information conveyed in them.

Among the many outside-of-the-family commercial sources, television is valued most for information. This research demonstrates that while Chinese children depend on TV, parents, and stores almost equally to learn about new products, they perceive TV as the most important of these. The highest ranking of TV implies that children are very emotionally involved with TV, probably due to the entertainment that it provides along with valued information. It may also be that many of the new products of interest to Chinese children are those from the West, and television provides this information through its increasing amount of programming and advertising that originate from Western sources.

Even though television is the newest of the mass media in China, it appears that the combination of its entertainment value and its information value is very appealing to children, so much so in fact, that they are willing to set aside their use of other media to a great extent. For example, those children who are heavy users of TV are less likely to read newspapers than moderate and light users. Either most of the children are trying to avoid the strictly educational tone of newspapers and magazines, or they feel that what they obtain from television is educational enough while being entertaining. From a functional standpoint, then, television alone seems to satisfy the needs of many Chinese children that are ordinarily met by the other media while meeting their predominant need for play.

What we see here is that the TV generation of China is here and now. The children regard it as an important new product information source more than any other medium, more than they do stores, and more than they do parents, grandparents, and friends — in a culture where the basic social unit is the family. Obviously, television is having an emancipating effect on China's children. It is reducing their reliance on traditional interpersonal sources of product information while catering to their need for entertainment. Consequently, television's central informational role makes it the most likely candidate as a communications channel for domestic and international marketing managers looking to target the children of China as consumers.

The paramount importance of television in the life of Chinese children requires that it be seriously examined. That is what the remaining chapters of this book do. They look at the interactions of children and television with an emphasis on television advertising specifically. This effort has not been undertaken before with such depth, but it is clearly needed by social scientists and business practitioners.

Appendix 2-1: A typical week of children's program on CCTV in January 2003

Channel	Monday	Tuesday	Wednesday	Thursday	Friday	Saturday	Sunday
CCTV-1	Sesame, Open the Door (15 min) Cartoon City (30 min) The Big Windmill (50 min)	Same as Monday	Same as Monday	Same as Monday	Same as Monday	Cartoon City (30 min) The Big Windmill (50 min)	The Second Start Line (50 min) The Big Windmill (50 min)
CCTV-4						Sesame, Open the Door (10 min)	Sesame, Open the Door (10 min)
CCTV-7	Cartoon City (30 min) Oriental Children (45 min × 3 times) Sesame, Open the Door (10 min) The Big Windmill (40 min) The Seven-piece Puzzle (10 min x 3 times)	Same as Monday	Same as Monday	Same as Monday	Same as Monday	Cartoon City (30 min) Oriental Children (45 min × 2 times) Sesame, Open the Door (10 min) The Big Windmill (40 min) The Seven-piece Puzzle (10 min × 2 times; 35 min)	The Second Start Line (50 min) 12th Studio (50 min) Oriental Children (45 min × 2 times) Sesame, Open the Door (10 min) The Big Windmill (40 min) The Seven-piece Puzzle (10 min × 3 times)
CCTV-8	Children and Youth Drama (45 min × 2 times)	Same as Monday	Same as Monday	Same as Monday	Same as Monday	Same as Monday	Same as Monday

Chapter 3

Children's Understanding of Television Advertising

We learned in Chapter 2 that children have many ways to encounter products and services. They may see the products being displayed in the shops, may learn about them from friends, classmates, and parents, and may see them presented in an advertisement. As the children are less able to read than adults, marketers often use television commercials to announce new products targeted at children. So, in China probably most children learn about new products and services from television commercials.

In Western societies there has been great concern among parents, public policy makers and marketers about the right to advertise products and services to young consumers. Based on theories and research developed by child psychologists and consumer researchers, we know that young children may not understand clearly the persuasive intent of advertising. Yet, they generally feel that television advertising is informative, truthful, and entertaining (e.g. Ward, Levinson and Wackman, 1972). As a result, parents and some consumer protection groups have argued that advertising to children may be unfair and unethical. In 1978, for example, the U.S. Federal Trade Commission proposed a ban on advertising to young children on the premise that it was unfair because they did not understand its intent. The proposal was supported by the American Academy of Pediatrics, the Child Welfare League, the National Congress of Parents and Teachers and the Consumers Union. However, strong opposition from the major television networks, toy makers and restaurant chains finally defeated the proposal. In some of the Scandinavian countries such as Sweden, advertising directed towards children under the age of 12 has been banned outright. And there is currently concern in the UK and some other European nations that what has been done in Sweden may be repeated in their economies as Sweden takes over some control of the European Common Market. Naturally, one might wonder if this movement might make its way to China where a quarter of the world's children live.

Robertson and Rossiter (1974) proposed five cognitive factors that directly related to children's ability to understand the purpose of television advertising and be able to defend themselves against its persuasive intent. The five factors included the ability to distinguish advertisements from programs, the ability to recognize a sponsor as the external source of the message, the ability to perceive the idea of an intended audience for the message, an awareness of the symbolic nature of commercials, and the ability to discriminate between products as advertised and products as experienced. They concluded that children who possess all these five cognitive abilities are able to recognize the persuasive intent of advertising, while children who do not possess them are more likely to associate an informative intent with advertising. As a result, these children are less able to defend themselves against advertising. A recent focus group study of 5–7 year-olds and 11–12 year-olds children provided empirical evidence that younger children possessed only some of the five abilities and saw more of an informative intent of advertising than older children (Mallalieu, Palan and Laczniak, 2002). The same study also proposed skepticism and evaluative judgements of advertising as additional factors that play a role in the development of children's ability to defend themselves against advertising's persuasive intent. This chapter will present some research findings that provide at least partial responses to Roberson and Rossiter (1974)'s thesis as it pertains to children in China.

Ways of measuring children's understanding of advertising

Underlying the issue of children's understanding of advertising are the methods used to measure it. Both verbal and non-verbal techniques have been used to access children's understanding of television advertising. When the verbal method is used, the child is typically asked to give an answer to questions such as "What is the purpose of television commercials?" or "What is the difference between a program and a commercial?". Such verbal methods were used by Ward (1972) and Ward, Wackman and Wartella (1977) in their landmark study of the topic. When a non-verbal method is used, a child is typically directed to watch a television program with commercials and then later asked what the commercial wants him or her to do. He or she may be asked to provide his/her answer by selecting a picture (Stephens and Stutts, 1982), or even by acting out the answer (Macklin, 1987). In Young's (2000) study, for example, children ages 4 to 9 years old were presented with television commercials with different endings and asked which ending should be used when a specific advertisement is shown on television. Three different endings were provided as alternatives: a fun ending option that presents the product in a bad light, a promotional option that sells the product, and a neutral ending that neither sells nor entertains. Macklin (1987) argued that non-verbal methods are more appropriate than verbal methods for young children because of their limited linguistics to verbalize their understanding.

Cognitive development and children's understanding of television advertising

In Western studies of child development, Piaget's (1970) theory of cognitive development has provided substantial guidance to research related to the communication process of advertising to children. The theory proposes that a child's ability to think and reason progresses through a series of distinct stages that are closely related to age. Integrating Piaget's (1970) stage theory of cognitive development and Selman's (1980) stage theory of social development, John (1999) proposes a model of consumer socialization that is shown to be particularly useful in characterizing children's responses to advertising. In the model, learning to be a consumer is a developmental process from the perceptual stage (3–7 years) to the analytical stage (7–11 years) to the reflective stage (11–16 years). In the perceptual stage, children can grasp concrete knowledge only. Their consumer knowledge is characterized by perceptual features and distinctions based on a single and simple dimension. They are egocentric and unable to take others' perspective into account. Children in the analytical stage are able to grasp abstract knowledge. Concepts are thought of in terms of functional or underlying dimensions. They are able to analyze marketplace information in two or more dimensions and have the acknowledgment of contingencies. They have developed new perspectives that go beyond their own feelings and motives, and can take a dual perspective of their own and that of others. Children in the reflective stage possess a multidimensional understanding of marketing concepts such as branding and pricing. They shift into more reflective ways of thinking and reasoning and focus more on the social meanings and underpinnings of the consumer marketplace. In terms of advertising knowledge, children in the perceptual stage can distinguish commercials from programs based on perceptual features such as length. Children in the analytical stage can distinguish commercials from programs based on persuasive intent. Children in the reflective stage are able to understand persuasive intent as well as the specific advertising tactics and appeals used in the commercials (John, 1999). John's theoretical framework, by combining that of Piaget and Selman, points in the direction of a positive effect of age on understanding of a social concept such as television advertising. Table 3-1 summarizes the three cognitive developmental models.

Most of the studies of children's communication processing of television advertising have supported these two theories. Studies have generally indicated that children's ability to distinguish programs from commercials increases with age (Meringoff and Lesser, 1980) as well as their comprehension of television advertising and its persuasive intent (Blosser and Roberts, 1985; Rubin, 1974; Ward, 1972). Some understanding of advertising intent usually emerges by the time most American children turn seven to eight (Bever et al., 1975; Rubin, 1974). Furnham (2000) reported that research among German children found that nearly two out of three 6-year-olds can make the distinction between programs and commercials, and can grasp the intent behind commercial messages. Chan (2000) surveyed 448 children in Hong Kong and found that children in grade 2 (aged 7–8 years) are beginning to know what advertising is and are aware of its persuasive intent. Using open-ended questions about the purpose of television advertising, thirty-one percent of children in kindergarten and seventy-eight percent of children in grade 3 reported that television commercials want people to buy things. Over

Table 3-1: Cognitive developmental models

Piaget's model of cognitive development (1970)	Sensorimotor (0–2 years) knowledge of the world depends on current sensory experience and activity; do not have the concept of object permanence	Preoperational (2–7 years) highly egocentric; believe what they perceive is real, do not have the concept of conservation	Concrete operational (7–11 years) can plan strategies and consider consequences, cannot think of actions in the abstract; fail to use the same principle in new situations	Formal operational (11–18 years) understand abstract principles, able to think of ideas apart from objects, still apply concrete strategy for problems not so experienced
Selman's model of social-cognitive development of perspective taking (1980)	Stage 0 (3–6 years) Undifferentiated and egocentric; unaware of others' perspectives	Stage 1 (6–8 years) Differentiated: aware of different perspectives in others	Stage 2 (8–10 years) self-reflective role taking; beginning to think from another's perspective	Stage 3 (10–12 years) third-person: simultaneously consider own and another's perspective	Stage 4 (12–15+ years) Societal: compare perspectives with social system
John's model of consumer socialization (1999)	Perceptual stage (3–7 years) grasp concrete knowledge only, focus on perceptual features, uni-dimensional, egocentric, unable to take others' perspective, can distinguish commercials from programs based on perceptual features	Analytical stage (7–11 years) understand abstract knowledge, think in terms of functional or underlying dimensions, analyze information in two or more dimensions, understand contingencies, dual perspectives, can distinguish commercials from programs based on persuasive intent		Reflective stage (11–16 years) more sophisticated understanding of marketing concepts, think and reason in more reflective ways, focus more on the social meanings of the marketplace, able to understand persuasive intent as well as the specific advertising tactics/appeals used in commercials

one-third of older children from grade 4 understood that television stations carry advertising for money. An experiment with 108 children in the U.K. found that none of the six-year-olds and a quarter of the eight-year-olds and a third of the ten-year-olds were able to understand the persuasive intent of television advertising (Oates, Blades and Gunter, 2002).

Research also suggests that by the age of nine children show marked improvement in understanding ambiguous wording, humor, and imagery found in advertisements (Belk, Mayer and Driscoll, 1984; Nippold, Cuyler and Braunbeck-Price, 1988). McNeal (1999) generalized these understandings under the term, consumer competence, and noted that it usually is in place by the age of 100 months. That is, even though they have much more to learn, children can be described as functioning consumers between the ages of 8 and 9 years old. Henriksen (1997) attempted to provide a detailed definition of understanding of advertising by differentiating three types of intent: 1) persuasive intent — that advertisements persuade, convince the audience to do something; 2) selling intent — that advertisements try to sell products or expect the audience to buy a featured product; and 3) profit intent — that the advertisers want to make money by selling goods. In a study of 112 children in kindergarten through fourth grades (ages 6–9), Henriksen found that children's understanding of advertising intent has a positive relationship with their perspective-taking ability, persuasive skill, and knowledge of buying and selling. The same study also showed that consumer dissatisfaction and co-shopping with parents play insignificant roles in predicting children's understanding of the purposes of advertising (Henriksen, 1997).

A meta-analysis was conducted to investigate the effect size of age on children's understanding of advertising intent. The estimated effect size based on 23 different studies of U.S. children with a total sample size of 2,934 was 0.37. However, the set of studies did not achieve homogeneity of effect size, indicating that there are study characteristics that have contributed to variance in the results. Further investigation indicates that significant study characteristics that influence the effect size include type of measurement of understanding (verbal vs. non-verbal), type of intent assessed (informational intent vs. persuasive intent), type of advertising exposure (no advertising exposure, exposed to program and commercials, and exposed to commercials only), and publication year. Effect size for verbal assessment was higher than that for non-verbal assessment. This is probably due to the higher demonstration of understanding of advertising intent among younger children when non-verbal assessment methods are used. Thus, understanding across ages would be more stable and the resulting correlation would therefore be lower. Effect size for persuasive intent was higher than the effect size for informational intent. This may be due to more consistent levels of understanding of informational intent across ages of children. The effect sizes for "no advertising exposure" and "exposed to program and commercials" are higher than the effect size for "advertising only." Seeing a commercial in isolation may cause confusion and thus a lower demonstration of understanding of advertising intent. Effect size for studies before 1974 is higher than effect size for studies conducted after 1974. The policies established in 1974 to protect children from advertising by prohibiting program-length commercials (programs that promote products within the body of the story) and host selling (the use of the same characters in commercials as are featured in adjacent programming) seem to have been successful in improving younger children's understanding of advertising intent. Thus, understanding across ages is more stable and a lower correlation results (Martin and James, 1997).

A study that measures Chinese children's understanding of television advertising: Purposes and methodology

As suggested in the forgoing literature review, most of the research on children's understanding of advertising has been conducted in Western societies. A research plan was developed during the winter of 2001–2002 to produce information about Chinese children's understanding of advertising and specifically television advertising that accounts for most of the advertising targeted to children in China. Believing that understanding might vary with the extent of exposure to advertising, three cities were selected to represent high, medium, and low levels of advertising development. Advertising development in this study is operationally defined as the percentage of national advertising in the year of 2000 (Fan, 2001). The three cities selected were Beijing, Nanjing, and Chengdu, whose advertising levels in 2000 were, respectively, 14.8 percent, 8.1 percent and 2.7 percent of the national advertising expenditure of 71 billion yuan (around US$8.7 billion). During a typical hour of afternoon programming to children the amount of advertising was around three minutes in Beijing (a city representing high advertising development), about two minutes in Nanjing (representing medium development), and also about two minutes in Chengdu (a city representing low advertising development).

The characteristics of the three selected cities are summarized below (China Infobank, 2003; China Advertising Yearbook, 2001):

	Beijing	Nanjing	Chengdu
City Population	13,830,000	6,240,000	10,199,000
Provincial population		73,550,000	86,400,000
City GDP (million yuan)	284,629	115,030	149,204
Provincial GDP (million yuan)		951,191	442,176
Per capita GDP (yuan)	20,581	12,933	5,118
City ad exp. (million yuan)	9,788		
Provincial ad exp. (million yuan)		5,398	1,786
Per capita ad exp. (yuan)	708	73	21
Number of TV channels (excluding cable)	CCTV (13) Beijing-TV (6)	CCTV (13) Nanjing-TV (6)	CCTV (13) Chengdu-TV (5)

The choice of these three cities located in different parts of China not only provided varying degrees of advertising development but also better representation of China in general as compared to single-city studies. For more details about the research methodology and questionnaires, please refer to Appendix 3-1.

Unlike in the U.S. where commercials in children's program hours are almost always targeted at children, we notice that children in China are exposed to an abundance of adults' commercials and relatively few children's commercials during children's programming. For example, in a typical television schedule of children's after-school programming of the national channel, CCTV-1, in May 2002, there were 85 commercials with an average length of around 11 seconds. Around 71 percent of these ads were commercials for adults' products while 29 percent were commercials for children's products. While we were not sure of the impact of these adult commercials, we felt that the situation might produce different degrees of children's understanding as compared to a situation where all the commercials are children oriented. Children in China may not perceive many advertising messages as messages for them but for their parents. Also, television program sponsorship is common in China (similar to the Public Broadcasting System in America, for example) where a company subsidizes program development and/or presentation. In a normal evening in May 2002, there were two subsidized programs. A subsidized television program usually starts with an announcement, "the following program is brought to you by.... (subsidizer)." There are separators between television programs and subsidizers' messages using billboards and voice-overs of the programs' names. We also were concerned with the impact of these sponsorships as compared to regular advertising on children's understanding of advertising.

Finally, we felt that regulation of advertising might control the quality of advertising to children and therefore indirectly influence their understanding of it. In our background search we found that although China's Advertising Law applies to the whole nation, there is some indication that the law is less strictly followed in provinces where advertising is less developed. For instance, among 66,824 illegal advertisements in all media examined by the State Administration for Industry and Commerce during the year 2000, two-thirds of them were from provinces with low advertising development (China Advertising Yearbook, 2001). Thus, children in high advertising development cities are exposed to more as well as higher quality television commercials which may have some impact on their understanding of advertising.

Understanding of television advertising by children was measured by a verbal method since it seemed that a number of studies and analyses of these studies suggested that verbal methods produced better results. Specifically, the children were asked three questions after a prefacing statement: When we watch television, some messages occur before or after the television program that are not related to the program. They are called commercials (*guanggao*). Children were then asked "What are TV commercials?", "What do commercials want you to do?", and "Why do television stations broadcast commercials?" For each question, several possible answers were presented. The children were asked to check one and only one answer that s-he thought was the most appropriate. The answers were developed based on the results of our focus group study of children conducted in Beijing (Chan and McNeal, 2002) and the research literature. Among all the answers presented in the first question, only one indicated participants' awareness of the persuasive intent of television advertising (i.e. television commercials are messages "to promote products"). For the second question, two of the five answers indicated participants' awareness of the persuasive intent of television advertising (i.e. television commercials want us "to tell our parents about it" and "to buy the products"). For the third question, two of the six answers indicated participants' awareness of the profit intent and the notion of program sponsorship (i.e. television stations broadcast commercials in order "to make money" and "to subsidize the production of programs"). These answers were classified as "demonstration of understanding" of television advertising. All other answers were classified as "not demonstration of understanding" of television advertising. The list of answers provided in the questionnaires and their classification into demonstration or not demonstration of understanding levels are summarized in Appendix 3-2.

Findings: A profile of Chinese children's understanding of television advertising: By age, gender, level of TV viewing, and level of advertising development

❏ *Understanding of television advertising and age*

Table 3-2 summarizes Chinese children's understanding of commercials by age groups. For the data analysis, children were categorized into four age groups, i.e. 6 to 7, 8 to 9, 10 to 11, and 12 to 14, representing the perceptual, early analytical, late analytical and reflective stages of John's (1999) model of consumer socialization, respectively. Since a substantial amount of research has shown some varying cognitive development

Table 3-2: Children's understanding of television advertising by age group (all answers)

| | Age group and cognitive stage (%) | | | | | | |
	6–7 N = 293 Perceptual	8–9 N = 507 Early analytical	10–11 N = 637 Late analytical	12–14 N = 293 Reflective	Total N = 1,730	Chi-square statistics	Spearman correlation
What are TV commercials?						91.6***	0.17***
Funny messages	15	11	11	8	11		
Messages for us to take a break	37	31	26	20	28		
Introducing products	29	25	21	28	25		
Promoting products@	16	29	41	43	34		
Don't know	2	4	1	2	2		
Total	100	100	100	100	100		
What do TV commercials want you to do?						71.6***	0.08***
Evaluate which commercial is good and which is poor	8	9	9	9	9		
Check the products at stores	20	25	18	19	21		
Tell parents about it@	34	27	21	16	24		
Buy the products@	33	33	49	53	42		
Don't know	6	5	3	3	4		
Total	100	100	100	100	100		
Why do TV stations broadcast commercials?						16.7	0.02
Not to waste time	16	16	14	11	14		
Help the audience	9	12	10	12	11		
Care the public	18	16	17	16	17		
Subsidizes the programs@	13	16	17	22	17		
Make money@	40	35	39	35	37		
Don't know	3	5	4	4	4		
Total	100	100	100	100	100		

*** $p < 0.001$.

Answers are in the order of their presentation in the questionnaire.

@ Answer(s) classified as demonstration of understanding of television advertising.

within the age range of 8–11, we split the analytical stage into two sub-stages (early and late analytical). This probe was permitted by a relatively large sample size in this age range. The results are displayed in Table 3-2.

Among all the children, 28 percent think that commercials are "some messages for us to take a break." Eleven percent perceive commercials as "some funny messages" and two percent report "don't know." About one quarter of the children think that television commercials are messages for "introducing products." There was a gradual increase in understanding of the promotional intent of commercials with age. However, even in the oldest group (ages 12–14), a majority of children still failed to demonstrate an understanding of the promotional intent of TV advertising.

For the question "What do commercials want you to do?", forty-two percent of children recognize that commercials "want people to buy the products." Twenty-four percent of the children think that commercials want them to "tell parents about it" and twenty-one percent report that commercials want them to "check the product at stores." Nine percent of children think that commercials are for them to "evaluate which commercial is good and which is poor" and four percent say they "don't know." Understanding of the selling intent of commercials increases with age of the children. Older children, those above ten, were more likely to understand that TV commercials want them to buy things or to talk with parents about the product advertised than younger children.

In response to the question "Why do television stations broadcast commercials?", Table 3-1 reveals that a high percentage of the children are able to identify the fact that television stations advertise to "make money" (37 percent) or that advertising "subsidizes the programs" (17 percent). Understanding of television stations advertising to make money is high even among the youngest children in the perceptual stage. One-sixth of the children think that television stations broadcast commercials in order to "care for the public" and eleven percent think that commercials "help the audience." Four percent of children say they "don't know." Contrary to the other findings, there was no improvement in understanding of "Why do television stations broadcast commercials?" among children of different age groups.

Table 3-3 summarizes the percentage of children demonstrating understanding of television advertising probed by the three questions by age group. Results show a general increase in understanding of "What are TV commercials?" and "What do TV commercials want you to do?" with age. However, understanding of "Why do television stations broadcast commercials?" did not increase significantly with age.

Correlation of the three questions about understanding of advertising is compiled in Table 3-4. Children's understanding of "Why do television stations broadcast commercials?" and "What do commercials want you to do?" shows a low correlation of 0.14. This indicates that the question "Why do television stations broadcast commercials?" may not be a core issue in the understanding of television advertising. Even if a child knows that television station carry commercials in order to make money, it does not mean the child understands the persuasive intent of advertising. In other words, awareness of a third party called "advertiser" does not mean an understanding of what the advertiser does.

Table 3-3: Children's understanding of television advertising by age group (answers classified as demonstration of understanding)

Demonstrate understand- ing of (%)	Age group and cognitive stage				Total	Chi- square statistics	Spearman correlation
	6–7 Percep- tual	8–9 Early analytical	10–11 Late analytical	12–14 Reflec- tive			
What are TV commercials?	16	29	41	43	34	73.0***	0.19***
What do TV commercials want you to do?	67	60	70	69	66	13.1**	0.05*
Why do TV stations broadcast commercials?	53	51	56	57	54	2.7	0.03

*   p < 0.05.
** p < 0.01.
***p < 0.001.

Table 3-4: Correlation of response to three questions on understanding of television advertising (answers classified as understanding or not understanding)

	What are TV commercials?	What do commercials want you to do?	Why do television stations broadcast commercials?
What are TV commercials?	1.0	0.17***	0.20***
What do commercials want you to do?		1.0	0.14***
Why do television stations broadcast commercials?			1.0

Standardized Cronbach alpha = 0.38.
*** p < 0.001.

❏ *Chinese children's understanding of television advertising compared to that of U.S. children*

Chinese children's understanding of television advertising shares some similarities as well as differences with U.S. children (see Table 3-5). We think that such comparison is meaningful since the U.S. study by Ward, Wackman and Wartella's study (1977) was a benchmark of its kind. We need to bear in mind that these two studies are both verbal based but differ somewhat in their methods of inquiry. The U.S. study used open-ended questions where answers were coded afterwards. Our study used close-ended questions where right and wrong answers were presented for children to choose from. The data are nearly thirty years apart. The principal similarity is the general improvement in understanding of advertising with age. Children's age has a substantial positive effect on their understanding of what television commercials are and their purposes. The sharpest increase seems to occur when the children move from the perceptual stage into the early analytical stage in the Chinese study, or roughly from kindergarten to third grade in the U.S. study.

Compared to children in the U.S., Chinese children have a higher understanding of why television stations broadcast commercials among

Table 3-5: U.S. children's understanding of television advertising by
grade level

	Grade level			
	K	3	6	Total
What are TV commercials?	N = 167	N = 199	N = 207	N = 573
Not demonstrate understanding[1]	94	75	59	75
Demonstrate understanding[2]	6	25	41	25
What do commercials want you to do?	N = 193	N = 200	N = 208	N = 601
Not demonstrate understanding[1]	96	85	62	81
Demonstrate understanding[2]	4	15	38	19
Why do TV stations broadcast commercials?	N = 140	N = 200	N = 207	N = 547
Not demonstrate understanding[1]	96	74	59	74
Demonstrate understanding[2]	4	26	41	26

[1] This refers to the percentage of children with low or medium understanding in the original table.

[2] This refers to the percentage of children with high understanding in the original table.

Source: Ward, Scott, Daniel B. Wackman and Ellen Wartella (1977), *How Children Learn to Buy: The Development of Consumer Information Processing Skills*, Beverly Hills, CA: Sage Publications, Inc., pp. 60–61.

all age groups. Twenty-six percent of U.S. children mentioned without aid that television stations broadcast commercials for money or for sponsoring programs while fifty-four percent of Chinese children were able to tell so when prompted. The fact that very young children show an understanding of why TV stations broadcast commercials may be a function of our research techniques. Teachers read out the possible answers, and they may have unknowingly emphasized "to make money." And it may be possible that the children were parroting what is heard so often in new China — make money!

In China, a child's age seems to have little effect on the child's understanding of why television stations broadcast commercials. Over half of the children, even at a very young age, are able to understand that television stations carry commercials to make money or to receive subsidies. Young Chinese children's understanding of the institutional function of television advertising (to sponsor TV program and to make money) deviates from Piaget's or Selman's model of cognitive development. As young children are supposed to be egocentric, they should be unable to see how advertising is related with other social systems such as the television stations. Perhaps what triggers their responses is the mentioning of "making money." This may be attributed to the drastic change in the media economy in the past two decades. Television stations that used to be the communists party's mouthpieces, began to broadcast mass entertainment and import programs to satisfy their audiences. Also, advertising on television has been growing rapidly, with expenditures doubling twice between 1996 and 1999 (ACNielsen Media International, 2000). To the mass audience, including children, there is an awareness of the sharp increase in the amount of commercials. We speculate that in emerging consumer societies such as China, children develop some understanding of the economic aspect of advertising as a result of public debates about the economic cost of advertising that logically arise in a quickly changing economic system.

Substantial television advertising and mass entertainment television programming are relatively new to China. Also, we believe that media literacy is not taught in elementary schools. So, it is surprising to find how much Chinese children do understand television commercials, particularly those residing in low advertising development areas. Although there is no study about how much media education takes place in the family, the results may suggest that Chinese parents who witness the commercialization of the Chinese media may teach their children about the economic issues of advertising, including the sponsoring of television programs. Result also indicated that less than 45 percent of older children ages 12–14 know that television commercials are messages to promote products. The low percentage also deviates from John's model of consumer socialization. Children in the reflective age are expected to have an understanding of the persuasive intent of advertising. We speculate that they may not because most of the commercials shown in Chinese children's program hours are not target at children. Further research is needed to explore reasons for such deviation.

However, over half of the younger Chinese children and over one quarter of the older Chinese children are unaware of "What are TV commercials?" suggesting that regulation of television advertising directed towards young children (9 years and younger) may be called for so that advertisers will not take advantage of the credulity of children.

❑ *Understanding of television advertising and gender*

Boys and girls demonstrate no difference in understanding of television advertising. When the age factor is controlled, boys do not have a better understanding of television advertising intent than girls or vice versa. This finding is what we might expect and is generally the case in Western societies.

❑ *Understanding of television advertising and level of TV viewing*

One may expect that a child spending more time watching TV will be expose to more television commercials, and hence have a better understanding of television advertising. In our study, television viewing was measured by asking children how many hours they watch television on weekdays and weekends. The total number of hours of watching per week was compiled and classified into nearly three equal groups of low, medium and high level of television viewing. Children in low, medium and high television viewing groups watch 3.5 hours or less, more than 3.5 hours to less than 11 hours, and 11 hours or more of television per week. Five percent of the sampled children who did not watch any television were classified in the low level of television viewing. We found that the partial Pearson correlation coefficients between television viewing and the understanding of "What are TV commercials?", "What do commercials want you to do?", and "Why do television stations broadcast commercials?" controlling for age are -0.01, -0.02 and -0.01 respectively. Thus, none of the partial Pearson correlation coefficients is significant at 0.05 level. In other words, when the age factor is controlled, children who watch television more often do not have a better understanding of television advertising intent. As amount of television viewing and children's understanding of television advertising are not related, any regulation ought to focus on the fairness of television advertising aimed at children, rather than on the sheer number of commercials per hour of children's programming as is done in the United States.

❑ *Understanding of television advertising and level of advertising development*

One might expect that children living in cities where advertising is highly developed will be exposed to more television commercials, and hence, have a better understanding of television advertising. Our evidence does not support this proposition. The partial Pearson correlation coefficients between level of advertising development and the understanding of "What are TV commercials?", "What do commercials want you to do?", and "Why TV stations broadcast commercials?" controlling for age are -0.06 (significant at 0.05 level), -0.01 (not significant at 0.05 level) and -0.14 (significant at 0.0001 level) respectively. The evidence suggests that contrary to what we expected, when the age factor is controlled, children residing in cities with low and medium level of advertising development seem to have a better understanding of television advertising intent than children residing in cities with high level of advertising development. There are two possible explanations. One is that in cities where advertising is less developed, advertising clutter is less severe. In such cases children will be less likely to avoid commercials and therefore, their understanding of commercials is higher. This explanation has the weakness as we have found that amount of television viewing has little impact on children's understanding of television advertising. Another possible explanation is that in cities where advertising is less developed, commercials are less regulated causing parents to be more concerned about the truthfulness of commercials. Consequently, they will be more likely to teach children how to identify deceptive commercials. As a result, children will have a better understanding of commercials. Children's responses indicate another possible reason. In cities where advertising is highly developed, there is a higher percentage of children believing that they are messages to help people. For example, fifteen percent of children residing in Beijing thought that television stations carry commercials in order to "help the audience" while only nine percent of Nanjing children and ten percent of Chengdu children think so.

We speculate that it can be attributed to the different amount of public service announcements (PSAs) that children exposed in different cities. An examination of a typical week of TV schedule in May 2002 indicates that there are 41 PSAs on CCTV-1 (7 in children's hour and 34 in the evening prime time). Beijing TV-1 carried more PSAs than CCTV-1. In the same week, there were altogether 63 PSAs (27 in children's hour and 36 in the evening). In the same week, there was not a single spot of PSAs broadcast in Nanjing TV-1 and Chengdu TV-1.

Further research is needed to examine how exposure to PSAs may have an impact on children's understanding of commercial and social messages broadcast on TV in cities with different level of advertising development. Further research is also needed to examine children's understanding of television advertising in other parts of China where advertising is far from developed, for example in the rural parts of China.

Some conclusions

In general, Mainland Chinese children show an increase in understanding of television commercials with age. Their understanding of why television stations broadcast commercials is higher than that of U.S. children. Over half of the sampled children, even at a very young age, are able to understand that television stations broadcast commercials in order to make money. Boys and girls do not differ significantly in understanding of television commercials. Children who watch television more often do not have a better understanding of television advertising intent. Contrary to what we expected, children residing in cities where advertising is less developed show a higher understanding of commercials.

Appendix 3-1: Methodology

Two elementary schools in each city were recruited to participate in the current study. School officials reported that students in these schools mainly come from the lower to middle classes. The total number of students in each school ranged from 800 to 1,700. Average class size ranged from 40 in Beijing and Nanjing, to 65 in Chengdu. For each school, we randomly selected one class from each grade (grade 1 through grade 6) to form the children sample. All aspects of the research procedure were conducted in the Chinese language (Mandarin). All the children were in the age group of 6 to 14. The children were asked to fill out a questionnaire in class. Children in grades 3 to 6 were instructed to complete the questionnaire on their own in the class. For children in grades 1 and 2, the researchers read out the questions as well as the answers, and ask the children to check the most appropriate answers. Students were assured that feedback was anonymous and there were no right or wrong answers for each question. Altogether, 1,758 questionnaires were collected from the children (460 from Beijing, 557 from Nanjing, and 741 from Chengdu). Several questionnaires were not usable because most of the questions were left blank or checked with two or more answers, leaving a net total of 1,744 usable questionnaires.

A draft questionnaire for the children was prepared based on Chan's (2000) study and a focus-group interview of twenty-two urban children ages six to twelve conducted in Beijing in October 2001. The questionnaire was then pre-tested in Beijing by personally interviewing eight children about its clarity. The questionnaire was revised and tested in Nanjing by personally interviewing eight children. After a subsequent round of revision, the questionnaire was finalized and distributed to school children in three cities. A doctoral student in psychology, a faculty member in the mass communication department, and a faculty member in the statistics department were utilized as researchers to coordinate the data collection.

The sample profile for children in three cities by city and grade, and by city and age are summarized below:

Grade	Beijing M	F	Sub-Total	Nanjing M	F	Sub-Total	Chengdu M	F	Sub-Total	M	F	Total
1	47	32	79	47	38	85	63	55	118	157	125	282
2	30	33	63	45	45	90	53	53	106	128	131	259
3	33	37	70	43	44	87	64	63	127	140	144	284
4	39	41	80	56	40	96	63	60	123	158	141	299
5	41	43	84	43	56	99	69	63	132	153	162	315
6	37	40	77	54	40	94	63	65	128	154	145	299
Total	227	226	453	288	263	551	375	359	734	890	848	1,738

Age	Beijing M	F	Sub-Total	Nanjing M	F	Sub-Total	Chengdu M	F	Sub-Total	M	F	Total
6	6	4	10	7	13	20	8	16	24	21	33	54
7	39	33	72	41	29	70	53	47	100	133	109	242
8	37	40	77	27	28	55	52	50	102	116	118	234
9	36	43	79	45	47	92	49	53	102	130	143	273
10	38	44	82	58	57	115	68	61	129	164	162	326
11	35	38	73	64	53	117	61	60	121	160	151	311
12	25	15	40	37	29	66	70	63	133	132	107	239
13	11	9	20	5	5	10	13	9	22	29	23	52
14				1		1	1		1	2		2
Total	227	226	453	285	261	546	375	359	734	887	846	1,733

Appendix 3-2: Questions and answers of children's understanding of television advertising

Q1. "What are TV commercials?"
Answers not demonstrating an understanding:
  "some funny messages";
  "some messages for us to take a break";
  "introducing products";
  "don't know"
Answer demonstrating an understanding:
  "promoting products"

Q2. "What do commercials want you to do?"
Answers not demonstrating an understanding:
  "evaluate which commercial is good and which is poor";
  "check the products at stores";
  "don't know"
Answer demonstrating an understanding:
  "want people to buy the products";
  "tell parents about it"

Q3. "Why do television stations broadcast commercials?"
Answers not demonstrating an understanding:
  "not to waste time";
  "help the audience";
  "care the public";
  "don't know"
Answer demonstrating an understanding:
  "subsidizes the programs";
  "make money"

Chapter 4

Children's Trust in Television Advertising

Chinese children have some understanding about the selling intentions of television advertising as was demonstrated in Chapter 3. For instance, most of them appear to know that television stations carry commercials for money and that the money goes to sponsor programs. In this chapter, we will examine Chinese children's *trust* of advertising that we operationalize as the extent to which they believe what is being said in television commercials, their criteria for making such judgements, and their perceptions towards advertised brands and non-advertised brands.

Advertising environment in Mainland China

One of the main determinants of children's trust of advertising is the nature of its environment. Children's advertising in China has several unique characteristics not shared by Western and more developed societies. First, while there is a great deal of advertising regulation in China, there is a lack of specific regulation of television advertising targeted to children. For example, in the United States there is regulation of the number of minutes of advertising per hour on week days and weekends that can be broadcast on television programming for children. That is not the case in China. We are going to discuss the regulation of Chinese children's advertisements in more detail in Chapter 9, but suffice it is to say that children-targeted advertising is not selected to any extent for specific regulations. Second, children in China have been exposed to a very high level of irresponsible advertising practices. China's advertising industry has developed rapidly since it introduced its reforms and open policies, but the industry has experienced a range of problems such as false advertising, inferior quality, and sub-standard advertising practices (Xinhua News Agency, 1995). Since the implementation of the

Advertising Law in 1995, local and central level officials of the State Administration of Commerce and Industry have prosecuted more than 160,000 illegal cases with fines totaling 450 million yuan, or about 58 million U.S. dollars (Xinhua News Agency, 2000). Ads for fake medicine, illegal medical services, and illegal food ads account for the biggest share of illegal advertising activities (Xinhua News Agency, 1998). Figure 4-1 shows an illegal print advertisement about a pill in a magazine for children and teenagers. In fact, the false advertising of pharmaceuticals has become so rampant that the Beijing Municipal Administration for Industry and Commerce, the watchdog of the advertising industry in Beijing, placed a 67-day ban on it in early 2002 (Hatfield, 2002). Some advertising to

Figure 4-1: An illegal print advertisement about a pill that claims to increase young people's height in a magazine for children and teenagers

children has been accused of misleading them and promoting unhealthy lifestyles (Zhou, 2001). For example, according to the China Consumers Association, food advertisers have claimed that certain biscuits can increase children's intelligence, certain health foods can enable students to score one hundred percent on examinations, and certain shoes can enhance growth. Some sales promotions even encourage children to consume excessively in order to obtain certain premiums or enter competitions (Luo, 2000). Much of television advertising in China is product-based rather than consumer-based. In Western countries there would be virtually no advertising of medical products to children since children are not equipped to understand such messages.

Third, the development of advertising is highly uneven within the nation. Children in different provinces have different level of exposures to advertising. In the year 2000, Beijing, Shanghai, and Guangdong province in the South were the country's three advertising centers, accounting for nearly half of advertising expenditures (Fan, 2001). There is a strong monopoly among the major advertising media. For example, China Central Television (CCTV) used to be the only television station covering the whole country. However, as more provincial television stations are able to broadcast programs nationally, CCTV's monopoly position has been threatened (Xinhua News Agency, 1998). In contrast, most of what U.S. kids see during children's TV hours is national advertising for children. That is, whatever children are seeing in California on the Cartoon Channel is the same as what they are seeing in New York or Chicago. Other than a small amount of local advertising for retailers, advertising on television programming that targets kids in the U.S. will be for children's products available in virtually any city and therefore are broadcast in virtually all cities simultaneously. But this is not so in China according to our own content analysis. In a typical week of children's programs on CCTV-1, we found there are 571 commercials and among which one third are for children's products. In the same week of children's programs on Beijing TV-1, we found 45 commercials and all of them are for adults' products. For Nanjing TV-1, we found 32 commercials and all of them are for children's products. For Chengdu TV-1, we found 28 commercials and one quarter of them are for children's products. We noticed that the total number of commercials carried by the national channel is between ten and twenty times that carried by local channels. Advertising clutter is surely a problem in children's programs in the national channel, but probably not a problem in many local channels.

Previous findings about trust in television advertising

Research in the Western societies indicates that by the age of eight, kids in the U.S. are able to understand, at least to some extent, advertising's persuasive intent and recognize the existence of deception in some advertising. Children ages eight and older no longer believe that "commercials always tell the truth" (Bever et al., 1975; Robertson and Rossiter, 1974; Ward et al., 1972; Ward et al., 1977). However, children from black and lower-income families are less discriminating (Bearden et al., 1979; Meyer, 1978). Beliefs about the truthfulness of advertising become even more negative as children move into adolescence. For example, the percentage of U.S. kindergartners, third graders, and sixth graders believing that advertising never or only sometimes tells the truth increases from 50 percent to 88 percent to 97 percent, respectively (Ward et al., 1977). In a national survey of over 500 British children aged 4 to 13, only six percent think that television commercials "always tell the truth," while 15 percent think they "quite often" are truthful (Greenberg et al., 1986). Most (60 percent) report that commercials "sometimes" tell the truth while the remaining 20 percent perceive commercials as "rarely or never" telling the truth. Perceived truthfulness of advertising appears not to depend on gender or social class of the children, but mainly depends on age. In general, the youngest children are most likely to believe that commercials tell the truth, while older children are more skeptical (Greenberg et al., 1986). Thus, in general, the younger the children the more they trust advertising. Critics of advertising to children would add that the younger the children are the more gullible they are and the more protection they need from advertising.

Closer to China, in a survey of 448 Chinese children in Hong Kong, the percentages of kindergartners and first graders, second and third graders, and fourth to sixth graders believing that commercials are mostly not true increase from 32 percent to 41 percent to 45 percent, respectively

(Chan, 2001). Boys demonstrate somewhat more growing skepticism of commercials with increasing school years than girls.

Focus group study of Chinese children's trust in television advertising

A focus group study was conducted in October 2001 in Beijing, China by the authors. Altogether three focus groups, consisting of 22 children, were interviewed. The three focus groups represented different age ranges of children (6–8, 9–10, and 11–12 years). All the children were from a school situated in the urban area near Peking University, and most were members of middle-income families.

When we asked children to what extent commercials are true, children from all age groups expressed some doubt about advertising content. Older children were more likely to think that television commercials lie. Younger children reported that they did not believe what commercials said if the visual presentation seemed not real. For example, a six-year old boy said, "A commercial shows a man coming out from a bubble. It is impossible. Therefore, it is definitely not true." A seven-year old girl said, "A commercial shows two men pushing a big boat. It is impossible and therefore, it is not true." Older children demonstrated more concerned about the truthfulness of advertising claims. A nine-year old boy mentioned, "Those medicine commercials that exaggerate its effects must be untrue. For example, a cold cure says you will recover immediately or within ten minutes. We know that all medicine takes at least one or two days to be effective. So, it must not be true."

Oldest children were also skeptical about sales promotions and other sales gimmicks. A twelve-year old boy said, "I think most of the commercials are untrue. They are so exaggerating. Especially if they tell you there is a big discount, you need to be cautious. Sometimes, they increase the price dramatically and give you a big discount. You probably don't gain anything." Another twelve-year old boy told us, "If a commercial promises that you can dial a toll-free number for information, you better watch out! Sometimes when you really make the call, they are going to charge you a very high telephone fee." Thus, across the age spectrum there was some mistrust of television advertising expressed in these three focus groups. We do not know if this mistrust extends to advertising in other media such as radio and magazines, but the children's vociferous responses within several discussions about television advertising causes us to think it does.

A recent study of Chinese children's trust of television commercials

Using the data from a large survey (described in Chapter 3) among 1,744 children, we find, as we did in the above discussed focus groups, that Chinese children are skeptical about television commercials (Table 4-1). A major portion of children (42 percent) perceives that half of television commercials are true. About ten percent and 19 percent think that "nearly all" or "most of" the commercials are true, respectively. On the negative side, ten percent believe that "nearly all commercials are not true" and 13.2 percent think that "most of the commercials are not true." The remaining 5.7 percent report they don't know.

Children's trust in television commercials differs with age. The percentages of children believing nearly all commercials are true or believing nearly all commercials are not true both decrease with age. With increasing age, children are more likely to believe that half of the commercials are true, or most of the commercials are not true. Thus,

Table 4-1: Children's perceived truthfulness of television advertising by age group and by sex

Television advertising is	Age group (%)				Sex (%)		Total (%)
	6–7	8–9	10–11	12–14	Male	Female	
Nearly all are true	16.3	11.6	8.3	4.5	10.0	9.7	9.9
Most are true	17.3	19.1	19.5	18.5	20.2	17.4	18.8
Half of them are true	30.2	39.8	47.6	46.9	39.4	45.5	42.3
Most are not true	9.8	12.4	13.4	17.5	12.6	13.6	13.2
Nearly all are not true	19.3	11.0	6.9	6.5	11.6	8.7	10.2
Don't know	7.1	5.9	4.2	6.2	6.1	5.1	5.7
Total	100.0	100.0	100.0	100.0	100.0	100.0	100.0
Chi-square statistics	86.6 ($p < 0.0001$)				10.3 (n.s.)		

Mainland Chinese children are not totally susceptible to advertising appeals. Even the very young children, those ages six to seven, express some doubt about the truthfulness of commercials.

Mainland Chinese children's perceived truthfulness of television advertising shows both similarities and differences when compared to children in the U.S. and in Hong Kong. Mainland Chinese children are similar to children in the U.S. in that with increased age there is a decrease in the percentage of children believing commercials are true. However, instead of doubting the truthfulness of most commercials, older Chinese children believe that half of the commercials are true and half of them are not. This is in contrast, for example, with the U.S. study by Ward et al. (1977) that found that 97 percent of sixth graders doubt the veracity of TV commercials. Only 21 percent of Mainland children ages ten think that mostly or nearly all television advertising are untrue compared to over twice, 45 percent, of Hong Kong children in Chan's (2001) study. Thus, while there is mistrust of advertising among Mainland Chinese children, it is not as great as that of children in the U.S. or Hong Kong.

We speculate, and research has shown, that in a newly emerging consumer market such as China, advertising is one of the important sources of information about products and services (McNeal and Ji, 1999). As Mainland children are in the process of learning to become consumers, they consider television advertising a valuable medium, so valuable in fact that they may not want to be critical or skeptical of it.

Similar to kids in the U.S., gender is not a factor in children's trust in television commercials. Boys and girls have similar beliefs about the truthfulness of television advertising.

Perceived truthfulness of advertising does differ with age and city of residence (see Table 4-2 and Figure 4-2).

Overall, children in Beijing perceive television commercials to be more truthful than children in Nanjing or Chengdu. Moreover, in all three cities, with increasing age there is a decreasing percentage of children that perceive "all commercials are true."

In John's (1999) model of consumer socialization, children are theorized to undergo a developmental process that proceeds through a series of stages as they mature into adult consumers. In other words, age

Table 4-2: Children's perceived truthfulness of television advertising by age group and city

City	Television advertising is	Age group (%)				Total (%)
		6–7	8–9	10–11	12–14	
Beijing		N = 80	N = 156	N = 155	N = 59	N = 450
	Nearly all are true	15.0	14.7	9.7	3.4	11.6
	Most are true	27.5	22.4	20.6	27.1	23.3
	Half of them are true	32.5	39.1	50.3	42.4	42.2
	Most are not true	8.8	9.0	11.6	8.5	9.8
	Nearly all are not true	8.8	9.6	1.3	8.5	6.4
	Don't know	7.5	5.1	6.5	10.2	6.7
	Total	100.0	100.0	100.0	100.0	100.0
	Chi-square statistics = 24.5, n.s.					
Nanjing		N = 91	N = 146	N = 231	N = 77	N = 545
	Nearly all are true	16.5	7.5	9.1	3.9	9.2
	Most are true	16.5	19.2	19.5	15.6	18.3
	Half of them are true	38.5	43.2	43.3	40.3	42.0
	Most are not true	9.9	11.6	13.4	23.4	13.8
	Nearly all are not true	13.2	10.3	10.0	7.8	10.3
	Don't know	5.5	8.2	4.8	9.1	6.4
	Total	100.0	100.0	100.0	100.0	100.0
	Chi-square statistics = 19.8, n.s.					
Chengdu		N = 124	N = 205	N = 250	N = 156	N = 735
	Nearly all are true	16.9	12.2	6.8	5.1	9.7
	Most are true	11.3	16.6	18.8	16.7	16.5
	Half of them are true	22.6	38.0	50.0	51.9	42.4
	Most are not true	10.5	15.6	14.4	17.9	14.8
	Nearly all are not true	30.6	12.7	7.6	5.1	12.4
	Don't know	8.1	4.9	2.4	3.2	4.2
	Total	100.0	100.0	100.0	100.0	100.0
	Chi-square statistics = 89.9, p < 0.0001					

of the children becomes a very significant factor in deciding their knowledge structures of marketplace information as well as their decision-making and influencing strategies as consumers. However, we find that in China the market environment (the residing city) also plays a significant role in the consumer socialization process. Children in Beijing, the city where advertising is most established, place more trust in

Figure 4-2: Children's perceived truthfulness of television advertising by age group and city

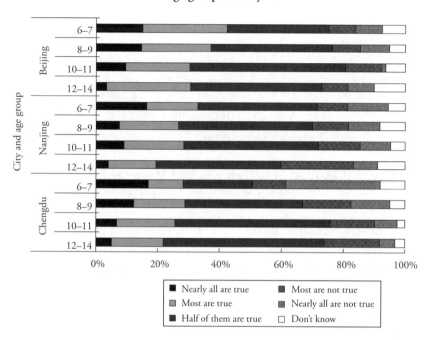

television commercials. Children in cities where advertising is less developed have a more skeptical attitude toward television advertising. There seems to be four possible explanations. First, children's beliefs may be attributed to the stricter advertising regulation standards maintained in the city where advertising is well established. Thus more global advertisers and foreign creative personnel are attracted to those cities and are well aware of and adhere to the advertising ordinances. However, in cities where advertising is not as well established such as Chengdu, advertising censorship may be loosely maintained and there may be more local advertisers using deceptive creative executions. As a result, the perceived credibility of television commercials among children in those cities is lower.

Secondly, as reported in the upcoming section, we find that a number of children say they'll check the products at the stores to see if commercials are true. As product distribution systems are less developed in second-tier cities like Nanjing and Chengdu, children may not be able to locate advertised products they want in the stores. As a result, they may think that commercials are untruthful. Thirdly, counterfeit products prevail in cities where advertising and marketing are less developed. Children are more likely to have purchased counterfeit products in those cities and will put the blame for their low quality or outright failure on the brand advertising. Consequently, they think that many commercials are not true. Fourthly, since advertising is rather new in those areas, Chinese children may mistrust it more, simply reflecting their mistrust of the unknown.

Do children who watch more TV put more trust in television commercials?

The answer generally is, no (see Table 4-3). The level of television viewing and perceived truthfulness of television commercials have no association in Nanjing and Chengdu. However, heavy TV viewers in Beijing are more likely to report that they do not know whether commercials are truthful or not. So, even though more television viewing means more experience with television advertising, it generally does not change the children's beliefs about the veracity of advertising.

Previous findings about "how do children know which commercials are true and which are not?"

Kindergartners are not able to explain why commercials lie whereas older children connect lying to persuasive intent (Ward et al., 1977). Most of the 7 to 10-year-old children admit that they have difficulties in detecting misleading advertising. Eleven to 12-year-olds children say they are able to use nuances of voice, manner, and language to detect misleading commercials (Bever et al., 1975).

Children's judgements about perceived truthfulness of TV advertising are based mostly on their perceptions of advertising content and their intrusive feelings. For those children who consider advertising to be mostly true, judgements do not differ by age. For those children who consider advertising to be mostly not true, their bases for judgements differ by age. The youngest children make their judgements based on others' opinions while the older children often base theirs on personal experiences. Bases for judgements do not seem to differ by gender (Chan, 2001).

Table 4-3: **Children's perceived truthfulness of television advertising by television viewing and city**

City	Television advertising is	Level of TV viewing (%)			Total (%)
		Low	Medium	High	
Beijing					
	Nearly all are true	12.1	11.0	11.7	11.6
	Most are true	26.7	21.3	21.7	23.4
	Half of them are true	35.8	47.6	43.3	42.1
	Most are not true	12.1	9.1	7.5	9.8
	Nearly all are not true	9.7	5.5	3.3	6.5
	Don't know	3.6	5.5	12.5	6.7
	Total	100.0	100.0	100.0	100.0
	Chi-square statistics = 19.2, $p < 0.05$				
Nanjing					
	Nearly all are true	7.6	10.9	9.1	9.1
	Most are true	18.2	18.2	16.7	17.9
	Half of them are true	39.1	48.4	39.4	42.4
	Most are not true	18.2	8.3	13.6	13.7
	Nearly all are not true	9.8	8.3	14.4	10.4
	Don't know	7.1	5.7	6.8	6.6
	Total	100.0	100.0	100.0	100.0
	Chi-square statistics = 14.6, n.s.				
Chengdu					
	Nearly all are true	11.3	10.4	7.9	9.8
	Most are true	15.7	16.3	17.7	16.6
	Half of them are true	36.5	45.2	44.8	42.3
	Most are not true	14.3	15.8	14.4	14.8
	Nearly all are not true	17.8	6.8	11.9	12.2
	Don't know	4.3	5.4	3.2	4.3
	Total	100.0	100.0	100.0	100.0
	Chi-square statistics = 17.5, n.s.				

Increased purchase and consumption experience, together with the developments in perspective taking that occur as children enter the reflective stage, facilitate the children's ability to associate advertising executions with deception. Family communication and control, peers, and television exposure also contribute to the development of skeptical attitudes toward advertising. For young children, critical attitudes seem to be furthered by parental control over television viewing (Soley and Reid, 1984) and less television viewing in general (Atkin, 1975; Robertson and Rossiter, 1974). Adolescents' skepticism toward advertising tends to be related to the development of independent thinking and access to alternative information sources. Higher level of advertising skepticism are reported by high school students who come from families that foster critical thinking and have access to alternative sources of information (friends), despite self-reports of heavy television viewing (Mangleburg and Terry, 1998). Students who conform to peer group norms are less skeptical about television advertising.

Current survey findings about "how do children know which commercials are true and which are not?"

From the survey that we conducted in China, children most often decide which commercials are true and which are not by trying the products or seeing if the products are from trustworthy brands or advertisers (see Table 4-4). About 18 percent of the children say they will check the products at the stores and 16 percent will ask their parents or teachers.

Table 4-4: How children know which commercials are true and which are not

Basis of judgements	Age group (%)				Total (%)
	6–7	8–9	10–11	12–14	
Try the products	21.8	34.5	26.1	23.2	27.3
See if they are about a trustworthy brand or they are by a trusted advertiser	13.6	19.0	31.3	30.8	24.6
Check the products at the stores	11.6	15.7	21.2	20.8	17.9
Ask parents or teachers	31.6	18.3	11.4	8.7	16.4
Whether the commercials seem so	12.9	7.3	7.9	13.1	9.6
See if endorsed by trustworthy persons	8.5	5.2	2.1	3.5	4.3
Total	100.0	100.0	100.0	100.0	100.0

Chi-square statistics = 160.6, p < 0.0001

Nearly ten percent of children rely on their intuitive feelings. Four percent will see if some trustworthy persons endorsed the products.

The bases for judging truthfulness of commercials do not differ by level of TV viewing, but differ by age among all three cities. The youngest children mainly depend on authorities to help the differentiation. As younger children typically cannot read, they simply cannot learn much about products from newspapers, magazines, and catalogues. Younger children thus learn to detect bias in television commercials mainly from their parents. Older children rely much less on authority. About 8.3 percent of the children, aged twelve to fourteen years old, often ask help from parents. Only 0.3 percent consults teachers or classmates. Older children mainly use their personal experience and trust in the brand/advertiser as bases for judgement.

In the consumer socialization of Mainland Chinese children, school teachers play an insignificant role. This is somewhat surprising since the children are so concerned with education, but we speculate that it is due to materialism being discouraged in Mainland schools. Most of the schools in China do not have a snack shop and students are encouraged to bring their own lunches and snacks to the schools. One of the moral guidelines for school-aged children as shown in Figure 4-3 is "Live a simple life. Don't be choosy in what you wear and what you eat. Don't spend money irresponsibly." Although sharing food and snacks and eating together with classmates, and exchanging consumption experience about new food products are common in schools (Guo, 2000), Chinese children seldom consult their teachers about truthfulness of television commercials.

Older children can read and can therefore access a wider range of sources for product information including newspapers and magazines. They also have more consumption experience to rely on to judge which television commercials are true. About one quarter of the older children told us they will try the advertised products or check the products at the stores. Older children, as consumers, are better able to compare user experience with advertising promises. Awareness of brands and the use of brand reputation for judging commercials become prominent when a child reaches age ten. One third of children age ten or above say they will see if the commercials are about a trustworthy brand or they are by

Figure 4-3: Photo of school rules

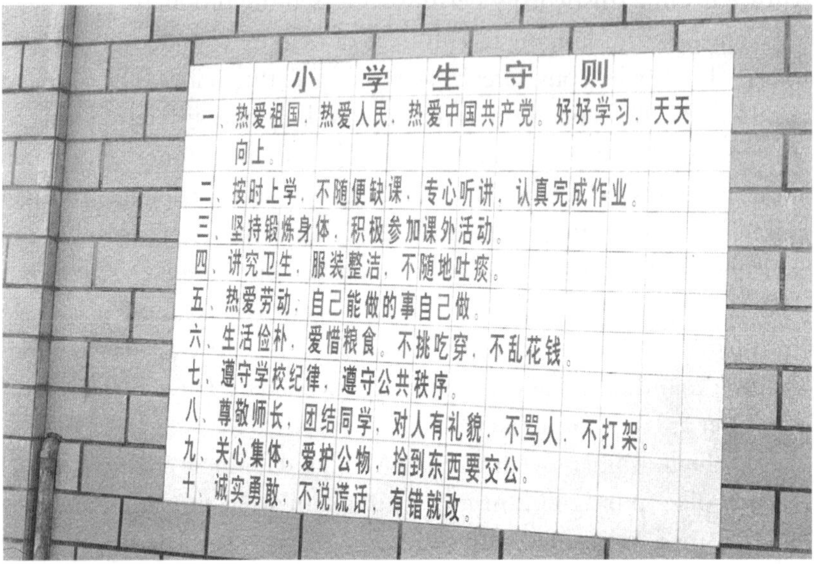

a trusted advertiser. This is consistent with John's (1999) model of consumer socialization stages. As the children enter the analytical stage, they are able to adopt a dual perspective (their own and that of the advertiser) and have a better understanding of brands.

The basis of judgement about advertising truthfulness does not depend to any extent on market environmental factors, but mainly on age. This indicates that processing of information about truthfulness is a cognitive and social developmental variable that is independent of the objective environment.

Current survey findings about children's perception of advertised and non-advertised brands

Very often marketers employ advertising to build up brand equity, or in other words, improve the overall image and perceived quality of the advertised products. Do children put more trust in advertised brands? We selected two product categories very familiar to children, a soft drink and a computer, to represent products with low and high involvement

Table 4-5: Children's perception of advertised and non-advertised brands

Perception	Age group (%)				Total (%)
	6–7	8–9	10–11	12–14	
Soft drink					
Advertised brand is better	24.4	24.8	27.9	20.6	25.2
Non-advertised brand is better	18.0	17.4	14.8	9.6	15.2
Equally good	27.8	19.6	13.4	8.6	16.9
Equally bad	9.2	7.9	3.6	3.4	5.8
Don't know	20.7	30.3	40.2	57.7	36.9
Total	100.0	100.0	100.0	100.0	100.0
	Chi-square statistics = 133.6, $p < 0.0001$				
Computer					
Advertised brand is better	26.7	28.3	33.8	28.5	30.1
Non-advertised brand is better	17.9	17.4	13.5	7.9	14.5
Equally good	30.4	25.5	17.0	11.3	20.8
Equally bad	8.8	5.9	3.1	1.4	4.6
Don't know	16.2	22.8	32.7	50.9	30.0
Total	100.0	100.0	100.0	100.0	100.0
	Chi-square statistics = 148.7, $p < 0.0001$				

level respectively, believing that trust would differ for them. We asked children what they think about the quality of an advertised brand vs. a non-advertised brand of each. The results of our queries are summarized in Table 4-5.

For both product categories, children have difficulties in giving a definite answer. Instead, they simply say they don't know. The confusion does not improved with age. In fact, the confusion increase steadily with age and there is a greater confusion for soft drink brands than for computer brands. Younger children aged 6 to 7 are more likely to perceive both brands as good. Confidence in advertised brands does not increase with age for both product categories, but confidence in non-advertised brand decreases sharply with age. There is a decrease in trust of non-advertised brands with age for both product categories. A small percentage of children view advertised and non-advertised brands as equally bad.

The concept of brand is certainly new in China as most goods are sold without branding. Contrary to what we expected, Chinese children do not demonstrate an increased understanding of brand equity with age. Older children are more likely to report that they do not know whether an advertised brand is better or a non-advertised brand is better. One possible explanation is that older children are more sophisticated in brand evaluation and will assess brands on more dimensions than younger children. If older children perceive an advertised brand to be better on some dimensions while a non-advertised brand is better on other dimensions, they may feel confused and cannot tell which one is better. Mainland Chinese children do perceive that, for high involvement products, advertised brands possess better quality. Therefore, advertisers and marketers of products and services requiring a high economic outlay should employ advertising to build up their brand reputations among children. Measures should be taken to enhance the quality perception of advertised brands in order to encourage repeat purchase.

Some conclusions

To conclude, a majority of Mainland Chinese children cast doubts on the truthfulness of television commercials. However, the mistrust is not as great as that of children in the U.S. or Hong Kong. Children's trust in television commercials tends to decrease with age. Boys and girls demonstrate similar beliefs about the truthfulness of television advertising. Children residing in cities where advertising is more developed put more trust in television commercials. The basis for judgement varies predominantly by age. Older children depend more on brand equity and user experience while the youngest children rely mainly on authority (i.e. parents or teachers). With increasing age, children are more confused about the quality of advertised versus non-advertised brands.

Chapter 5

Children's Attention to and Liking of Television Advertising

It was concluded in Chapter 4 that Chinese children have limited trust of television advertising. Older children, particularly, place less trust in commercials than younger children and rely less on authorities in making such judgements. Consequently, he or she is not sure whether advertised brands or non-advertised brands are better. In this chapter, we are going to explore: (1) children's liking of commercials; (2) their preferences for different types of creative executions; (3) their attention to commercials; and (4) their responses to their most favorite and most disliked commercials. We will also examine how children's attention, liking and trust in advertising are related.

Do Chinese children like television commercials?

Previous studies indicate young children like commercials very much. But as a child grows in her or his ability to recognize deception in advertisements, together with an understanding of advertising's persuasive intent, the liking of commercials drops drastically (Robertson and Rossiter, 1974; Rossiter and Robertson, 1976). For example, the percentage of U.S. children liking all commercials decreases from 69 percent for first graders to 56 percent for third graders to 25 percent for fifth graders (Robertson and Rossiter, 1974). Other studies demonstrate a similar pattern of downward trends in liking of advertisements from the early elementary school grades to high school (Chan, 2001; Lindquist, 1978; Moore and Stephens, 1975).

However, children seem to like certain type of commercials. For instance, in a survey of children age 9 to 10 in Belfast, Northern Ireland, most of the children said they enjoyed particular commercials, especially those featuring humor (Collins, 1990). In one of our focus group studies of urban Chinese children in Beijing, children became very excited during their reports when we asked them about their favorite commercials and why they liked them (Chan and McNeal, 2002). Three boys in the age group 11 to 12 voluntarily sang jingles from the commercials and two boys in the age group 9 to 10 even acted out their favorite commercials. From our focus group studies we found that younger children like funny commercials, commercials with a jingle and commercials for products they liked. According to a seven-year old boy, "I like a commercial of a health food called 'Naobaijin' (means brain's platinum). It shows an eyeball jumping out. It is so funny." A nine-year old girl told us that she likes a jelly commercial. The commercial says, according to her, "A jelly that you can suck." Later she told us that she likes the commercial because the jelly tastes good.

Older children like funny, but meaningful commercials including public service announcement ads. These ads are often about environmental protection, protecting the ozone layer, and industrial safety. A ten-year old girl said, "I like a commercial about shooting birds. The bird is singing happily on a tree and a man tries to shoot it. The bird says, "We are friends and why should you do this to me?" I like this commercial because we should protect birds." An eleven-year old boy declared, "I like a series of commercials by a brand of cold cure. In the birthday party, people all sing and ask the girl to make a wish. She sneezes and all the candles are blown off. In another commercial, a man wins a lottery. But after a sneeze, the lottery ticket is gone forever. I like these commercials because they are so funny." These are the words of a twelve-year old girl, "I like a commercial about safety at the construction sites. I learn from the news that many workers are hurt in the construction sites. The commercial reminds people to take precautions to protect their lives. I think it is meaningful."

When we ask children in the focus group what sorts of commercials they don't like, children at all ages said they don't like commercials that are slow, long, and repetitive. Additionally, older children pointed out that they don't like commercials that exaggerate and make false claims. A six-year old boy told us, "I don't like a computer commercial. I am enjoying my favorite cartoon program and the commercial interrupts it. The commercial is boring and it doesn't have a lot of actions." A nine-year old boy followed with, "I don't like a vitamin commercial. It is awful and exaggerating. At the end of the commercial, it says 'Buy one and get one free. You'll become double beautiful.' How can a person become double beautiful? It is meaningless." Finally, an eleven-year old girl complained that commercials make the program run too long. A one-hour program becomes one and a half hour with the commercials, according to her. Sometimes it becomes so late, she told us, that her mother doesn't allow her to watch. So, she cannot finish her favorite program.

What a survey found about children's liking of commercials?

Based on the focus group results described above, we conducted a survey in three major cities of China — Beijing, Nanjing and Chengdu — that is described in detail in the Appendix to Chapter 3. Children's liking of television commercials in the three Chinese cities we surveyed are displayed in Table 5-1. It shows that almost one-third of the 1,744 respondents (31 percent) hold neutral feelings towards television commercials. Just over 24 percent of children say they like television commercials and 9 percent say they like them very much. About 20

Table 5-1: Children's liking of television advertising by age group and by sex

What is your feeling towards TV commercials	Age group (%)				Sex (%)		Total (%)
	6–7	8–9	10–11	12–14	Male	Female	N=1,744
Dislike very much	22.9	17.4	12.3	11.6	18.9	11.9	15.4
Dislike	21.2	18.1	21.1	21.8	19.8	21.3	20.3
Neutral	19.9	24.3	35.0	44.0	30.6	31.0	30.8
Like	18.9	27.0	26.3	20.5	21.6	26.7	24.2
Like very much	17.2	13.2	5.2	2.0	9.0	9.1	9.2
Total	100.0	100.0	100.0	100.0	100.0	100.0	100.0
Chi-square statistics	124.9 (<0.001)				18.7 (<0.001)		

percent of children say they don't like television commercials and 15 percent say that they don't like them very much. Thus, among all the 1,744 children questioned, approximately one-third like commercials, one-third don't, and one-third neither like nor dislike them. The rather high noncommittal percent is of concern to us, not knowing how informative it is.

Liking of television commercials differs with age. In all three cities, the extent of strong feelings (either "dislike very much" or "like very much") towards television commercials both decline with age. Chinese children do not demonstrate an increase of disliking of commercials with age, as they do in the United States. Instead, the youngest children hold very strong feelings about commercials. They either like commercials very much or dislike them very much. Older children, on the other hand, express indifference to television commercials. To advertisers, this can be both good news and bad news. It is good to know that disliking of commercials decreases with age. But it is bad to know that children lose the kind of interest or enthusiasm toward television commercials when they grow up. It will surely be more difficult to persuade audiences who are less involved with television advertising. Liking of television commercials also differs with gender. Girls tend to report liking commercials more than boys.

Children residing in the three different cities of Beijing, Nanjing and Chengdu, which have different levels of television viewing, enjoy commercials to different extents (see Table 5-2). Overall, children in Beijing liked television commercials more than children in Nanjing and Chengdu. The percentages of "like" and "like very much" for children in Beijing, Nanjing and Chengdu are 41 percent, 29 percent, and 32 percent, respectively. There is no consistent pattern between level of television viewing and liking of commercials. However, children who watch less television seem to dislike commercials more. It may be that those who don't watch television very much dislike it, in general, including commercials and programming.

Girls in Nanjing and Chengdu like television commercials more than boys. However, both boys and girls in Beijing like television commercials to similar extents.

Children's liking of television commercials varies among heavy TV

Table 5-2: Children's liking of television advertising by city and by television viewing

What is your feeling towards TV commercials	City (%)			Level of TV viewing (%)			Total (%)
	Beijing	Nanjing	Chengdu	Low	Medium	High	N=1,744
Dislike very much	11.4	20.3	14.2	17.5	12.0	17.0	15.4
Dislike	16.4	18.9	23.9	21.5	19.5	19.8	20.3
Neutral	31.3	31.7	29.9	27.5	33.3	31.6	30.8
Like	28.4	20.5	24.4	23.3	27.5	21.9	24.2
Like very much	12.5	8.6	7.6	10.1	7.7	9.6	9.2
Total	100.0	100.0	100.0	100.0	100.0	100.0	100.0
Chi-square statistics	37.3 (<0.001)			17.2 (<0.05)			

viewers and light viewers. But there is no consistent pattern in the relationship between level of television viewing and liking of commercials in the three cities. In Nanjing, heavy TV viewers dislike television commercials more than light viewers. In Chengdu, a reverse pattern is found. Light viewers in Chengdu dislike television commercials more than heavy viewers. In Beijing, there is no significant difference in liking of commercials for light, medium and heavy television viewers. It is difficult to explain these inconsistencies. More in-depth research on a city by city basis might highlight the differences.

Which creative executions do they like and don't like?

There is little research on how much children know about specific advertising tactics and appeals. Advertising knowledge of a more specific form emerges much later in the developmental sequence as children approach early adolescence (Boush, Friestad and Rose, 1994; Friestad and Wright, 1994; Paget, Kritt and Bergemann, 1984). Younger children (ages 7–8) consider advertising primarily as a conduit of product information. Older children (ages 10–11) are able to analyze the creative content and identify some execution tactics (Moore-Shay and Lutz, 1997). Among various types of advertising tactics, children easily identify celebrity commercials as they express liking of commercials using famous characters (Chan, 2000). Advertising creative personnel working in China propose age specific tactics for Chinese children. For example, commercials targeted at younger children should provide immediate pleasure while commercials for older children should show how the brand could help them to meet challenges and master their environment (O'Hanlon, 2000).

Based on our focus group interviews with children in Beijing, we identified five types of creative executions that children have expressed some feelings of either like or dislike. These five types include funny commercials, animated commercials, public service announcements (PSAs), commercials that increase knowledge, and commercials with celebrities. From our conversation with kids in Beijing, it seems that they demonstrate conflicting views toward commercials using celebrities. For example, a nine-year old boy said that a commercial endorsed by a famous person will be more trust-worthy. However, a twelve-year old boy thought otherwise — he said that famous people are paid to endorse a product.

In our large-scale survey, we asked children to rate commercial execution on a three-point scale (1 = dislike, 2 = neither like nor dislike, 3 = like). "Don't know" cases were dropped. Table 5-3 summarizes mean scores for the five types of television commercials by age and by sex. Children's responses to the five types of commercials differ considerably. Children rank "commercials that increase our knowledge" as their most favorite type of commercials, followed by "funny commercials," then "public service announcements" and "animated commercials" that are tied for third place. "Commercials with celebrity" is the least favorite type of creative execution. In general, children express liking for four out of the five types of commercials. They tend to have neutral feelings toward commercials with celebrities.

Children of all age groups like commercials that increase their knowledge. This supports the well known thinking that Chinese children have a high aspiration for knowledge. One may argue that they are giving socially acceptable answers to interviewers in China. However, this at least indicates that possession of knowledge is a socially preferable norm in Chinese societies. Therefore, it is suggested that advertisers package

Table 5-3: Children's response to different types of commercials by age group and by sex

Type	Overall mean*	s.d.	Age group						Sex			
			6–7	8–9	10–11	12–14	F-value	p	Male	Female	F-value	p
Commercials that increase our knowledge	2.9	0.4	2.9	2.9	2.9	2.9	2.3	n.s.	2.9	2.9	1.1	n.s.
Funny commercials	2.8	0.6	2.7	2.8	2.8	2.7	2.6	<0.05	2.7	2.8	8.9	<0.01
Public service announcements	2.6	0.7	2.3	2.6	2.7	2.8	26.3	<0.001	2.6	2.6	0.2	n.s.
Animated commercials	2.6	0.7	2.7	2.7	2.6	2.5	8.5	<0.001	2.6	2.6	0.2	n.s.
Commercials with celebrities	2.1	0.9	2.2	2.1	2.0	2.1	5.0	<0.01	2.0	2.2	25.4	<0.001

ANOVA test of difference of overall mean: F-value = 349.9, $p < 0.0001$

* A higher score indicates higher level of liking on a scale from 1 to 3.

n.s. = Not significant at 0.05 level.

or instill knowledge in their commercials to make them more appealing to Chinese children and probably to their parents, too.

Liking of the other four types of creative execution differ by age. Surprisingly, children ages 6 to 7 do not enjoy funny commercials as much as older children. There is also an increase in liking of public service announcements with age. On the other hand, the liking of animated commercials decreases with age. There is a slight drop in liking of commercials with celebrities across age groups. Boys and girls have different responses to "funny commercials" and "commercials with celebrity" but not the other commercials. Girls like "funny commercials" and "commercials with celebrity" more than boys.

Implications for advertisers

Based on Chinese children's liking of different types of commercials, we suggest the following age specific advertising strategies:

- For very young children (those under 7): They have difficulties in understanding humor that is presented. They love animation. They like celebrities. Commercials targeted at them should be straightforward, visually stimulating, and with animated characters. Animated characters tend to be more friendly, funny and playful to young children, and tend to get and keep their attention so that messages are more likely to be received by them.

- For children aged 8 to 11: They enjoy funny commercials and probably are able to understand visual and verbal humor. They still enjoy animated commercials, but to a lesser extent than the younger children. Probably animated characters could be employed with this group as long as the message is age-graded accordingly. Also, these middle-age children start to appreciate public service announcements, probably because they find them meaningful. In fact, this may be the earliest age group at which PSAs can be effectively presented. However, they are not as interested as younger children in commercials with celebrities. So, there is probably little need to utilize celebrities in PSAs as is common in the West. Generally, commercials targeted at this age group should be funny, demonstrate a caring about society and the environment, and be straightforward.

- For children aged 12 to 14: They enjoy public service announcements more than funny commercials. They have lost some interest in animated commercials and they are no longer interested in commercials with celebrities. The children in this age group generally have taken on a serious relation with ads. Thus, commercials target at this age group should be meaningful, caring about the society and the environment, and use much less animation. Giving them a sense of accomplishment and acceptance among peers will be appealing.

How do children react to their favorite and most disliked commercials?

In a survey of adults in China, 85 percent of the respondents said their favorite commercials make them change attitude towards the brand. On the other hand, 67 percent said their most disliked commercials make them feel "that couldn't be me in the commercial" (Kovarik, 2001). In our survey, we ask children how they react to their favorite commercials and to their most disliked commercials. We gave them four choices and allowed them to choose more than one. Table 5-4 summarizes their responses by age and by sex. Close to sixty percent of children say their favorite commercials make them want to see the commercials again. Close to half of the children associate liking of commercials with development of a good brand image. Over one third of the children want to buy the product right away and twenty-nine percent project themselves into their favorite commercials.

Similarly, over seventy percent of children say their most disliked commercials make them not want to see the commercials again. Close to half of the children associate disliking of commercials with development of a bad brand image. Over one-third of the children do not want to buy the product and only twenty-seven percent project themselves into their most disliked commercials and "feel that couldn't be me."

Children's responses to their most favorite and most disliked

Table 5-4: Children's response toward their favorite commercials and most disliked commercials by age group and by sex

Response	Age group (%)						Sex (%)			
	Total	6–7	8–9	10–11	12–14	Chi-square	p	Male	Female	Chi-square	p
My favorite commercial made me …											
want to see it again	57.8	66.9	54.8	57.3	54.6	13.1	<0.01	55.0	60.4	5.3	<0.05
have a good impression about the brand	48.1	43.9	44.2	46.5	62.5	30.1	<0.001	47.5	49.0	0.4	n.s.
want to buy the product right away	35.5	43.6	36.5	32.1	34.1	12.0	<0.01	38.3	32.9	5.3	<0.05
feel "that could be me"	29.0	41.6	29.8	27.4	18.1	40.6	<0.001	28.2	29.8	0.5	n.s.
My most disliked commercial made me …											
don't want to see it again	70.5	70.8	68.7	71.8	70.9	1.4	n.s.	68.9	72.1	2.1	n.s.
have a bad impression about the brand	43.5	43.7	42.7	39.4	53.4	16.2	<0.01	45.9	41.3	3.7	n.s.
don't want to buy the product	33.4	50.8	30.7	32.0	24.0	54.2	<0.001	35.3	31.5	2.9	n.s.
feel "that couldn't be me"	26.5	52.2	27.4	19.2	14.7	138.4	<0.001	27.6	25.1	1.4	n.s.

n.s. = Not significant at 0.05 level.

commercials vary somewhat among different age groups. Children of all age groups say their most disliked commercials make them not want to see the commercial again. Older children less often associate attitudes toward the commercials with intention to purchase. They also less often project themselves into commercials they like or dislike a lot. Increase in age, however, is related with a stronger link between attitudes toward the commercials and impressions toward the brands. In other words, older children more often develop good impressions about particular brands through their favorite commercials.

Boys and girls respond to their favorite commercials differently. After seeing their favorite commercials, girls more often say they want to see the commercials again. Boys more often say they want to buy the product right away.

Children's response toward their most liked and most disliked commercials indicates that Chinese children are quite realistic. Only one third of the children relate liking and disliking of commercials with immediate purchase intention. The link between liking specific commercials and impulse to purchase decreases with age, indicating that older children are more detached from television commercials. We can see it by the sharp decrease in children's projection into commercials they like or dislike a lot with age.

The increase in the association of impressions toward brands and attitudes toward commercials suggests that brands could build a good relationship with the young consumers through advertising activities. While short-term promotional activities may be useful and important to younger children, thematic activities should be used to establish long-term relationship and brand loyalty among older children.

How often do children watch commercials during commercial breaks?

Even if television commercials are presented in a creative and funny way, children may not pay any attention to them. Commercials must impinge upon children's consciousness in some way before they can have any effect. Previous studies indicate that there are basically three ways of measuring children's attention to television commercials: by asking children whether they watch them, by asking parents whether children are watching, and by direct observation of children during the commercial breaks. Some scholars consider direct observation of children more valid because the other two methods suffer from recall error and difficulties in monitoring others' viewing behaviors (Gunter and McAleer, 1997). Parents in the U.S. report that children demonstrate a drop in attention to commercials compared with the attention to the program preceding the commercials (Ward, Levinson and Wackman, 1972). By using experimental studies (e.g. Wartella and Ettema, 1974) and in-home observation (e.g. Ward and Wackman, 1973), it was found that younger children's attention to commercials is often affected by perceptual characteristics of commercials such as the loudness of the jingle. Older children's attention to commercial is often affected by the content of commercials.

There are no consistent findings regarding study of children's attention to commercials at different age groups. For example, a study in the U.S. found that older children pay less attention to commercials as they talk more during the commercial break and become more negative toward advertising (Ward, Levinson and Wackman, 1972). Some studies have reported an increase in attention with age. In an observational study that recorded attention in family homes, children up to 10 years old watch commercials only 40 percent of the time, while 11- to 19-years-old watch them 55 percent of the time (Bechtel, Achelpohl and Akers, 1972). Some studies have reported no difference by age when children are asked how often they watch television commercials when they are on (Chan, 2001; Greenberg, Fazal and Wober, 1986). A study found that girls pay greater attention to commercials than boys while another study found no difference in attention between boys and girls (Chan, 2001). A previous study concluded that attention to television commercials depends on personal factors and stimulus factors. Personal factors include parental and peer influence, the level of motivation, and attitudes toward commercials. Stimulus factors include the nature of the television program, the content of the commercial, and the product being advertised (McNeal, 1987).

In our survey, we used the self-reporting method in measuring children's attention to television commercials. We asked children how often they watch television commercials. Table 5-5 summarizes the results by age of children and shows that attention to commercials varies among children. Twenty-nine percent say they switch to other channels nearly every time. Over fifty percent of children say they watch television commercials sometimes. The percentages of 'watch often' and 'watch nearly every time' are both small.

There is a general decrease in attention to television commercials with age, with the exception of a high level of switching channels among very young children. Over one third of young children ages 6 to 7 say they switch channels nearly every time. As previous studies indicate, young children's attention to television commercials is influenced mainly by perceptual characteristics of commercials. These findings suggest that commercials broadcast in China are not perceptually stimulating or attractive to young children. The high percentage of children at all age groups switching channels or paying little attention during commercial breaks should be of concern to marketers and advertisers. To parents and policy makers, this low attention to television commercials by the very young may be good news in that the adverse effects of television advertising on children will be undermined.

Overall, boys and girls pay more or less the same attention to television commercials. However, girls demonstrate a drop in attention with age, while boys do not. For example, nine percent of girls 6 to 7

Table 5-5: Children's attention to television advertising by age group

When commercials are shown on TV, you will ...	Age group (%)				Total (%) N = 1,744
	6–7	8–9	10–11	12–14	
switch to other channels nearly every time	35.4	25.2	26.5	34.2	28.9
watch sometimes	43.9	53.9	55.2	51.7	52.1
watch often	9.9	11.8	9.8	6.8	9.8
watch nearly every time	10.9	9.1	8.5	7.2	9.0
Total	100.0	100.0	100.0	100.0	100.0
Chi-square statistics	23.2 (<0.01)				

watch nearly all commercials while only four percent of girls 12 to 14 watch nearly all. Interaction of age and television viewing has influence on children's attention to commercials. Both low and medium television viewers do not report a drop in attention with age. However, heavy television viewers report a significant drop in attention with age.

Attention, liking and trust of television commercials

Do children put more trust in commercials if they like them? Do children more often watch commercials if they like them? Do children more often watch commercials if they trust them? A previous study indicates that perceived truthfulness of commercials is positively related with liking of commercials. Children who put more trust in commercials like them more (Chan, 2001).

The Pearson correlations between children's attention to, liking of and perceived truthfulness of television commercials in this current study are shown in Table 5-6. A positive correlation was found between attention and perceived truthfulness. Children who put more trust in commercials are more likely to watch them (or vice versa). Again, a positive correlation is reported between attention and liking of commercials. Children who like commercials are more likely to watch them during the commercial break. For marketers and advertisers, making a commercial that children like is utmost important because if they like it, they will watch it again and again. Moreover, if they like it, they probably will believe it.

Perceived truthfulness and liking of television advertising also show a positive correlation. Children who put more trust in television

Table 5-6: Pearson correlation coefficients of attention, liking and perceived truthfulness

Pearson correlation	Attention	Liking	Perceived truthfulness
Attention		0.36***	0.19***
Liking			0.32***
Perceived truthfulness			

*** $p < 0.001$.

commercials also like them more (or vice versa). Perhaps this represents the group of children most easily persuaded by selling messages. Media education on critical reading and viewing of persuasive messages is mostly needed for this audience segment. The implication for marketers is that commercials should be judged credible in order to gain a good impression from children.

Some conclusions

The study reported in this chapter illustrates Mainland Chinese children are losing much of their interest in commercials when they grow up. Perhaps this is due to them having exposure to different channels of communications about products and services as they get older. They may get increasingly used to advertising and become indifferent toward commercials in general. Girls like commercials more than boys, although there appears to be no simple explanation for it. Children in Beijing enjoy commercials more than children in Nanjing and Chengdu. This may indicate that liking of commercials is related with the level of advertising development. A previous study indicates that children's liking or disliking of television advertising is mainly based on its entertainment vale (Chan, 2001). In areas where advertising is more developed, we expect that there will be more global advertisers, employing creative talents that make the commercials more appealing and entertaining. As a result, the creativity level of advertising will be higher. There is no consistent pattern between TV viewing and liking of commercials. Children at different ages enjoy different creative executions. Marketers should therefore employ advertising strategies that are most appealing to the age group they are targeting. Mainland Chinese children are quite realistic. They seldom purchase a particular product just because they like its commercial. There is a general decrease in attention to television commercials with age. However, the youngest children switch channels very often. Girls and heavy television viewers demonstrate a significant drop in attention with age. Significant Pearson correlations are found among attention, liking and perceived truthfulness. Children who like the commercials more are more likely to watch them, and also trust them more. Marketers should therefore make their commercials interesting and credible in order to increase their effectiveness. Perhaps pretesting the commercials among children would allow advertisers to improve their quality and therefore their viewing.

Chapter 6

Parent-Child Communication about Consumption and Advertising

It was shown in Chapter 5 that Chinese children's liking of advertising generally decreases with age. They like most those commercials that increase their knowledge. It also was demonstrated that their attention, liking and perceived truthfulness of television commercials are positively correlated. Obviously, among many consumer behavior patterns *parents* play an important role in children's learning about advertising and forming feelings about it through parent-child communication, training, and modeling (Ward et al., 1977). In this chapter, we will look at how Chinese parents communicate with children about consumption, and how parent-child communication patterns differed among different demographic groups and different dyadic relationships.

Demographic profiles of Chinese parents

The one-child policy, first adumbrated by China's Premier, Deng Xiaoping, in a 1979 speech, was in place nationwide by 1981. The "Technical policy on family planning" followed two years later. Still in force today, the technical policy requires intrauterine devices for women of childbearing age with one child, sterilization for couples with two children (usually performed on the woman), and abortions for women pregnant without authorization. The principal modification of the one-child policy occurred in the mid-eighties when, in response to rising levels of female infanticide, the government relaxed the policy in the countryside for couples whose first child was a girl. In many parts of China this has developed into a de facto two-child policy, as rural officials found the selective enforcement of a mixed policy — one child for couples whose first child was a boy, two children for couples whose first child was a girl — difficult to manage (Mosher, 2001; Population Research Institute, 2001).

According to official statistics, the one-child policy has been largely followed in the urban cities of China. For example, among all the babies born in 1990 in Beijing, 87 percent are single children. Among all the babies born in the same year in Shanghai, 86 percent are single children (Liu and Liu, 1996).

Fines instead of forced sterilization or abortion were used later on as a means to maintaining the one-child policy. In 1989, the Provincial People's Congress set up the penalties: couples will be fined 1,500 yuan (almost US$200) for the first extra baby, and 3,000 yuan for the second, with an additional 1,500 yuan fine for each extra child (Zhang, 1999). The fines have been increased year by year and based on one's wealth, and therefore are much higher today. For example, recently a news report from *Lu zhong News* (2002) stated that 500 thousand yuan were charged to a Shandong couple who are going to have a third child.

One aim of the provincial population policy is to encourage couples to delay their marriages. People who get married below the state-specified minimum age are subject to fines. Reproductive couples wanting to have babies should be approved first and given a birth permission certificate (*zhunshengzheng*). All couples must have the certificates before the wives get pregnant.

As the Chinese population policy encourages late marriages, Chinese parents are usually in their late twenties or early thirties when the first baby arrives. Table 6-1 shows the breakdown of the major household types in Mainland China. The average household size in 1995 was 3.7. According to official statistics in 1995, sixty-nine percent of children live with their parents alone forming nuclear families. Twenty-three percent of children live with parents and grandparents, seven percent of children live with a single parent (most likely a mother), and one percent of children live with grandparents only. In the Chinese society, grandparents and grandchildren sometimes form a household when the parents go to others cities for work.

Mainland Chinese parents are unique in two ways that have major consumer behavior implications for their children. Firstly, they can only have one child in the family and therefore they have high expectations

Table 6-1: Distribution of family household types in China

Family household types	Percentage
One-person	5.9
One-couple without children	9.3
Husband-wife with children	58.0
Single parent with children	5.9
Grandparents and grandchildren only	0.7
3+ generation	19.4
Others	0.8

Source: 1995-mini census, cited in Zeng (2002).

of their children. There are "no second-chance" parents. If their parenting fails, that is, their children fail to fulfill their expectations, they cannot hope for a second child to make up for it. Consequently, Chinese parents feel they must invest heavily in their children in order to get a good return from them as adults. Secondly, the current generation of singletons' parents, men and women born in the late 1960s and 70s, has suffered from severe material shortages and political turmoil (Davis and Sensenbrenner, 2000). As the new era of economic reform has instituted a reward system based on formal education and qualifications, these parents want their lost past to be compensated for by a better future for their second generation (Zhao, 1996). The parents are the lag-behinds in the consumer revolution in China introduced in the 1990s. And it shows. In a survey in Beijing, Chinese children considered television to be the most important information source to learn about new products, not their parents as once was the case (McNeal and Ji, 1999).

When explaining Chinese perspectives towards parenting styles, Confucianism is a Chinese ideology that has been widely investigated by Chinese and Western researchers. Some major concepts of Confucianism that have been considered include: supreme moral person (Lei, 1993; Metzger, 1992); filial piety (Hsu, 1981; Kelly and Tseng, 1992); social harmony (Domino, 1992); collective decision making (Stander and Jensen, 1993); good manners, and particularly the importance of education (Ekblad, 1986; Ho, 1989). All of these notions have significant consumer behavior implications for children and family.

Chinese parents are highly motivated to exert control over their children because of their intense concern for their children to attain high academic achievement. Parents stress that children should learn in a variety of different ways such as doing supplementary exercises, private tutoring and attending music and language lessons. Parents strongly feel that school achievement is a means of bringing honor to the family and is the only ticket for a successful life. Consequently parents are willing to sacrifice and save money in order to facilitate children's study. Different from the Western style of authoritarian control that tends to be related with parental rejection and hostility, Chinese parental control is usually accompanied by a very supportive and warm parent-child relationship (Chao and Sue, 1996).

The implications of all these Confucian-based studies suggest that Chinese parents are very concerned about the school achievement and moral behaviors of their children, and they stress control as well as family harmony. In a study of Chinese children in Hong Kong, for example, children reported that their parents use television commercials to teach them about restrictive consumption behaviors (for example they should not drink wine or take illegal drugs) and desirable moral behaviors such as protecting the environment (Chan, 2001).

How do parents influence children?

In the family, parents can influence children's consumer behaviors in three ways (Ward, Wackman and Wartella, 1977):

By acting as role models: Children observe and learn from their parents' behavior, even though sometimes parents may not always be aware of it. The learning experience is very important when the child is small and unable to make independent purchases. For example, a child sees the mother pinch her nail on an apple to check if it is fresh, and from this observation he or she learns how to tell whether a fruit is ripe. Similarly, a child observes how the mother reads through the newspapers, cuts the sales coupons, and presents them during a shopping trip. When a child accompanies the mother to the store, he or she observes how the mother interacts with the sales personnel, what sort of questions she ask, and how she compares prices of different brands at the same store or at different stores. Thus, probably most of the consumer behavior patterns initially learned by children are copies of those of their parents, particularly mom.

By discussing with children: Parent-child communication about consumption can be initiated by the children or by the parents. When a child initiates the interaction, often it is when he or she makes a purchase request. When the parents initiate the interaction, it is often because they want to teach the child something. That something may be related with consumption behavior or it may be related with other issues that concern them. For instance, in our conversation with parents in China, they told us they sometimes talk with their children about healthy eating habits when they see commercials for snacks.

By monitoring and controlling children's consumption behaviors: When children are small, they rely heavily on the parents to provide them with money and opportunities to choose favorite products. In this way, children gain personal experience in consumption behavior. As the children grow, they are more likely to develop their own sources of income and additional sources of information and increasingly shop independently. Parents can still control children's consumption behavior by restricting their sources and amounts of income and by specifying what can and cannot be bought. Parents can also encourage desirable behaviors through rewards, punishments and debriefing discussions with children after their purchases.

A study of parental roles and influence in China

Together with the survey of school children in three cities in China (described in Appendix 3-1), we also conducted a survey of their parents. The purpose of the study was to explore these questions:

1. How do Chinese parents communicate with their children about consumption?
2. How does culture influence the family communication patterns?
3. Do family communication patterns vary with demographic characteristics of the parents and the children?

Procedurally, we ask the school children sample to take a question-naire home to either their parents for completion. Questionnaires were then returned to the schools and gathered by the teachers who passed them on to the research team. Altogether 1,758 questionnaires were distributed to the school children and 1,700 questionnaires were returned (437 from Beijing, 525 from Nanjing, and 738 from Chengdu). Thirty-five questionnaires were not usable because most of the questions were left blank or checked with two or more answers, leaving a total of 1,665 usable questionnaires. The response rate was 94.7 percent.

The questionnaire treated four topical areas: (1) parent-child communication regarding consumption and advertising; (2) the frequency with which parents watch TV and discuss commercials with children; (3) parents' attitudes toward advertising in general and toward advertising targeting specifically at children; and (4) parental control of television viewing. Demographic information was collected also. For ease of reading we will include findings regarding the first two areas in this chapter and findings of the third and fourth areas in the following chapter.

The sample profile as summarized in Table 6-2 shows that the sample contains slightly more females. Most of the surveyed parents are in the age group 30–39 with a very small percentage of young mothers, perhaps due to the Party's control over when women can be pregnant. Also, the table shows that about one third of the parents have high/technical school education level, one quarter are college level (less than four years), and one quarter are university level (four years or more). Most of the surveyed children belong to the lower-middle class living in households with monthly incomes of 1,000–5,000 yuan.

How do parents and children communicate about consumption?

Classifying family communication patterns provides a way of assessing the interaction between parents, children, and their media and consumption environments. Family communication has been conceptualized as being composed of two dimensions (see Moschis, 1987 for a review). The first dimension, *socio-orientation*, refers to the vertical or relationship-oriented patterns of communication. The emphasis is on parental control and children's deference to authority. The second

Table 6-2: **Sample profile of parents (N = 1,665)**

Demographic	Number	%
Sex		
Male	684	41.8
Female	953	58.2
Age		
20–29	30	1.8
30–39	1,337	80.9
40–49	224	13.6
50–59	61	3.7
Education		
Junior high or below	324	19.5
High/technical school	569	34.2
College	360	21.6
University	412	24.7
Occupation		
Government officials	182	11.1
Senior managers/administrative	120	7.3
Professional and technical staff	217	13.2
General clerical/sales	237	14.4
Workers	394	23.9
Teachers/researchers	190	11.5
Self-employed/private sectors/ freelance professionals	167	10.1
Farmer/others/unemployed	139	8.4
Monthly household income		
No income/1,000 yuan or below	489	30.4
1,001–2,500 yuan	735	45.6
2,501–5,000 yuan	289	17.9
5,001 yuan or above	98	6.1

Cells may not add up to total due to missing cases.

dimension, *concept-orientation*, refers to issue-oriented communication. The emphasis is on the establishment of an independent evaluation of an issue by the children. The two dimensions give rise to a four-category typology consisting of what are termed, laissez-faire, protective, pluralistic, and consensual parent-child communication (Figure 6-1).

Figure 6-1: Four types of family communication patterns

Socio-oriented communication

	Low (mean <= 3.5)	High (mean > 3.5)
Low (mean <= 3.0)	*Laissez-Faire* Little communication with children; Little parental impact on consumption 24.5% of Chinese parents 22.1% of U.S. parents	*Protective* Stress vertical relationships, obedience and social harmony; Children have limited exposure to outside information 24.4% of Chinese parents 23.4% of U.S. parents
High (mean > 3.0)	*Pluralistic* Stress horizontal relationships; Issue-oriented communication; Children are encouraged to explore ideas and express opinions 12.8% of Chinese parents 27.3% of U.S. parents	*Consensual* Maintain control over children's consumption; Frequent communication with children about consumption 38.3% of Chinese parents 27.3% of U.S. parents

(left margin, vertical label: Concept-oriented communication)

Source for U.S. parents: Rose et al. (1998).

Laissez-faire parents are neither concept- nor socio-oriented. They seldom communicate with their children about consumption and also have the least control over their children's consumption behaviors. *Protective* parents express a high level of socio-oriented and a low level of concept-oriented communication. They emphasize obedience and social harmony, and do not encourage children to develop independent preferences. *Pluralistic* parents demonstrate a low level of socio-oriented and a high level of concept-oriented communication. They maintain a relatively horizontal parent-child relationship and encourage children to express their ideas. Finally, *consensual* parents practice a high level of both socio-oriented and concept-oriented communication. They encourage expression of ideas but at the same time maintain high parental control over children's consumption behavior.

Empirical studies indicate that there are cultural differences in family communication patterns. American mothers, as a group, emphasize independence and individualism more than Japanese mothers, who emphasize social harmony and respect for authority (Power et al., 1992; Itoh and Taylor, 1981). American mothers more often engaged in concept-oriented communication about consumption than Japanese mothers, and Japanese mothers more frequently employ socio-oriented communication patterns. As a result, Japanese mothers are classified primarily as either laissez-faire or protective. American mothers are distributed relatively equally across the four groups (Rose et al., 1998).

We expect culture to play a significant role in parental style and patterns of family communication. Using Hofstede's (1991) framework, different societies show a significant difference in five cultural dimensions, including individualism/collectivism, power distance, uncertainty avoidance, masculinity/femininity and long-term/short-term orientation.

Individualism/collectivism refers to a country's cultural position with respect to the importance of the individual or the group. The concept of *power distance* captures the desire within a society for hierarchy versus egalitarianism. *Uncertainty avoidance* is a society's tolerance for ambiguity. While *masculinity* stands for a preference in society for accomplishments, heroism, assertiveness, and material success, *femininity* refers to a preference for relationships, modesty, caring for the weak, and the quality of life (Hofstede, 1983; 1998). We feel that uncertainty avoidance and masculinity/femininity dimensions are not directly related to family communication patterns, while the difference in the power distance and the individualism/collectivism dimensions will affect the family communication patterns.

Power distance mainly refers to the extent to which less powerful members of a society accept that power is distributed unequally (Hofstede, 1980). China has a long history of being an authoritarian society that emphasizes Confucius's five cardinal relations between sovereign and minister, father and son, husband and wife, old and young, and friends (Yang, 1959). Chinese people have a strong respect for authority (Bond, 1991). In the traditional Chinese family, children are expected to show absolute obedience to parents and should not express conflicting ideas openly. Therefore, we expect that Chinese parents will engage in a high level of socio-oriented communication.

The individualism dimension refers to the degree to which individual decision making and actions are encouraged by a society. In an individualistic society, everyone is entitled to his or her own opinion (Hofstede, 1980). Therefore, self-sufficiency and independence will be related with the individualism dimension. The implication in the family communication setting is that parents will treat children as individuals and are willing to involve them in family purchase decisions. However, collectivism deals with group ties and stress on social harmony. Recognizing that Chinese parents put emphasis on collectivistic values, we expect that Chinese parents will engage in a low level of concept-oriented communication.

From the survey data we collected from parents, the parent-child communication patterns are summarized in Table 6-3. Chinese parents report a medium to high level of socio-oriented communication (mean = 3.6 on a scale of five) as we expected. A mean value of one represents parents that very seldom engage in socio-oriented communication while a mean value of five represents parents that very often engage in socio-oriented communication. Chinese parents say that they often or very often control the type of products children can or cannot buy. The three statements with the highest means are all about restrictions on choice of product categories. Also, the table shows that parents are eager to know how children spend their allowance, and they speak out when children buy things they do not like.

The level of concept-oriented communication reported by Chinese parents is medium (mean = 3.0 on a scale of five), meaning that parents sometimes engage in concept-oriented communication. Contrary to what we expected, Chinese parents do not engage in a low level of concept-oriented communication. Chinese parents very often solicit children's preferences when they buy gifts for them. Fifty-one percent of parents often or very often allow children to decide things to buy. Parents say that they sometimes discuss with their children about consumption and places to buy things. However, parents seldom consult children or ask them for help when buying things for the family, and post-purchase

Table 6-3: Parent-child communication about consumption, watching television with children and discussion about commercials

Items	Often/very often (%)	Sometimes (%)	Seldom/ very seldom (%)	Overall mean	S.D.
Socio-oriented communication				*3.6**	*0.7*
I tell my child he/she is not allowed to buy certain things.	70.0	23.9	6.1	3.8	0.9
I tell my child what things he/she should buy.	67.3	23.0	9.6	3.7	1.0
I tell my child not to buy certain things.	66.2	25.2	8.6	3.7	0.9
I want to know what my child did with his/her money.	54.6	24.1	21.3	3.4	1.2
I complain when I do not like something that my child bought for him/herself.	50.6	32.2	17.3	3.4	1.1
Concept-oriented communication				*3.0**	*0.6*
I ask my child his/her preference when I buy something for him/her.	75.7	17.8	6.6	4.0	1.0
I let my child decide which things he/she should or shouldn't buy.	50.7	34.0	15.3	3.4	1.0
I talk to him/her about where different products can be bought.	43.3	29.8	26.9	3.1	1.2
My children and I talk about buying things.	32.8	38.4	28.7	3.0	1.1
I ask my child about things that I buy for myself.	27.0	37.7	35.3	2.8	1.2
I ask my child for advice about buying things for the family.	25.9	35.3	38.8	2.8	1.2
I ask my child what he/she thinks about things that he/she buys for him/herself.	28.2	29.2	42.7	2.7	1.2
I ask my child to help me buy things for the family.	12.4	44.6	42.9	2.5	1.0
Co-viewing				2.8	0.9
Watch television with children on weekdays	17.9	20.0	62.1	2.2	1.2
Watch television with children on weekends	50.9	31.5	17.6	3.4	1.1
Discuss about TV commercials					
Discuss TV commercials with children	14.8	33.6	51.7	2.4	1.1

* Socio-oriented communication is significantly higher than concept-oriented communication (t = 33.9, p < 0.0001).

discussions about children's consumption experience is low. Parents more often use socio-oriented communication than concept-oriented communication.

We notice that there seems to be some contradictory findings: over two third of the parents said they tell their children what things they should not buy while at the same time fifty percent of parents said they let their children decide which things they should or should not buy. Our interpretation is that Chinese parents have strict control over what type of products children can or cannot buy while at the same time allowing children some freedom in choice of brands for products that they are allowed to buy. This reflects a compromise of an autocratic approach to parenting and complete freedom for children in purchase decisions. The parental control on the product category persists even when children become older. Although we did not ask what sort of products and services are not acceptable for the children, based on Zhao's (1996) study and our focus group study in Beijing, we expect that sensitive products such as tobacco and alcoholic drinks, and products that distract children from study are prohibited. Products enhancing and facilitating intellectual growth are encouraged. This suggests that marketers should therefore position products and services target at children in such a way that they are appealing or at least acceptable to parents. For example, electronic games need to be perceived as creative and educational by parents before they can get access to children and be presented as fun and exciting. Food or snacks need to be perceived as healthy and energy-giving or else parents will not allow children to buy them.

The medium level of concept-oriented communication about consumption indicates to a certain extent that Chinese parents do not perceive themselves as competent consumers. They seldom hold discussions with their children about consumption experiences. The demographics of the family communication patterns sheds light on why parents hesitate to engage in consumption related communication with children. In the subsequent section, we will find that educational level and household income level are positively related with the amount of concept-oriented communication. We expect that parents with low education or low income are more likely to be price-conscious and less global. They will be less informed about current market environments and less familiar with new products. As a result, their children may perform an opinion leader role in the family.

Family communication patterns are classified into four parental types through median splits on the socio- and concept-oriented dimensions of communication (see Figure 6-1). One quarter of the parents is protective and another one quarter is laissez-faire. One-sixth of the sample is pluralistic while nearly forty percent is consensual. Compared to a U.S. study (Rose et al., 1998), Chinese households contain a higher proportion of consensual and a lower proportion of pluralistic parents than those in America.

Chinese parents report high control of type of products children can or cannot buy. Therefore marketers who target children should build a good relationship with parents first. For products acceptable to parents, advertising efforts should put emphasis on establishing brand preferences among children by directly advertising to them.

How do family communication patterns vary demographically?

Parents' use of socio-oriented or concept-oriented communication varies with their demographics. Overall, high levels of economic status (high household income, high education level and professional occupations) are associated with concept-oriented communication. Parents with high economic status are more likely to involve children in purchase decisions by asking their preferences and asking about their feelings after purchases. Mothers more often use socio-oriented communication than fathers. Communication with sons and daughters do not differ significantly in spite of the emphasis in China on the male child. Parent-child communication also varies with age of children. Use of socio-oriented communication decreases when children get older. Parents of children ages 6–11 engage in a similar degree of socio-oriented communication while parents of older children ages 12–14 use socio-oriented communication less often. While all parents are still eager to know how children spend their money, parents of older children give less instruction on what the children should buy and less often make comments if the children buy something they don't like. Parents of older children more often report that they ask children to help buy things for the family. In other words, as children grow older, they enjoy a greater autonomy in consumption, encounter less restriction from parents in buying things, and participate more in family purchase decisions. Since, we did not survey children aged 14 and above, we cannot tell whether this observed trend in parent-child communication continues as the children move to adolescence and become young adults, but we expect it.

Watching TV together and discussing television commercials

When parents and children talk about consumption, it is natural that the conversation will involve the sources of information about products and services. As television advertising is a major source of product information — perhaps the most important source (McNeal and Ji, 1999) — parent-child communication often includes comments about television commercials. Watching television with children and discussing commercials with them can be active ways of teaching children how to process information in the commercials. Topics of discussion can be divided into two types. General comments are about television commercials as a category, e.g., "commercials always lie," or "you cannot buy everything you see advertised." Specific comments are about a particular commercial, e.g., "that commercial is too scary," or "you should learn to respect your elders, just like the girl in this commercial." (Ward, Wackman and Wertella, 1977).

In the survey of parents, we ask them how often they watch TV with their children on weekdays, and on Saturdays and Sundays. We also ask them how often they talk with their children about the contents of TV commercials. They could check on a five-point scale from very seldom to very often. The results are summarized in Table 6-3.

Nearly two-thirds of all parents report that they seldom or very seldom watch TV with their children on weekdays, according to the table. Co-viewing becomes more frequent during weekends. Fifty-one percent of all parents report that they often or very often watch TV with their children on Saturdays and Sundays. Parents seldom discuss commercials with their children they see on television. Only about one-sixth of all parents report that they often or very often talk with their children about advertisements.

Watching television with children depends on demographic characteristics of parents and ages of children. Parents' status (education, household income, and professional occupations) is negatively correlated with co-viewing. Parents of lower educational level and with lower household income, workers and self-employed parents are more likely to watch television with their children. Parents with children ages 6–7 seldom watch TV with them while parents with children ages 12–14 more often watch TV with them. Watching television with children involves time and interest. Parents with high economic status probably can't afford the time to do so. Also, parents of younger children may not have the interest to watch with them because of the nature of the television programs. Co-viewing with older children may indicate that parents are more concerned about what sort of programs their children are watching and the possible influence from the media. Co-viewing does not depend on sex of children. Surprisingly, fathers report more co-viewing with children than mothers.

Discussion of television commercials with children does not differ among most of the demographic groups of parents. Parents' occupation is the only characteristic that makes a difference in the discussion of commercials. Parents engaged in professional and administrative occupations, teachers and researchers are more likely to discuss with their children about television commercials. Discussion about commercials also does not depend on demographic characteristics of children. Parents of older children do not report more or less frequent discussion of commercials with their children.

Parent-child interaction and understanding of television advertising

Some scholars predict that parents can increase children's understanding of the purpose of commercials by talking with them about commercials (Ward, Wackman and Wartella, 1977). In our study, we do not find evidence to support this notion. We compiled Pearson correlation between parent-child discussion of television commercials and those children's understanding of commercials (using the three questions reported in Chapter 3). None of the correlation coefficients was significant. We think that the lack of association between discussion and children's understanding may be due to two reasons. Firstly, when Chinese parents discuss commercials with children, the emphasis is not about teaching them what commercials are and educating them about the purposes of television advertising. The emphasis is more on expressing parents' attitudes toward television commercials in general and on teaching their children what things they can or cannot buy. Secondly, due to the time pressure of parents, and to some extent on the children too, the discussion of television commercials with children may be too little to create any significant influences.

Parent-child interaction and children's attitudes toward television advertising

We also compiled Pearson correlations to examine whether watching TV with children and discussing commercials with children have any impact on children's attitudes toward commercials. Children's attitudes toward television commercials were measured in terms of two dimensions: liking of commercials and perceived truthfulness of commercials, as reported in Chapter 4. Watching television with children was found positively correlated with children's liking of commercials ($r = 0.10$, $p < 0.001$) and children's perceived truthfulness of commercials ($r = 0.06$, $p < 0.05$). These results suggest that the more frequently parents watch TV with children, the more likely children develop positive attitudes toward television commercials. Discussing commercials with children however has no relations with children's liking or trust in commercials. The finding seems a bit conflicting. Further research is needed to explore what is being discussed in parent-child's communication about television commercials.

Some conclusions

Our survey results indicate that Chinese parents overall, possess a high level of socio-oriented communication and medium level of concept-oriented communication. Chinese parents are classified primarily as consensual type with both high socio- as well as concept-oriented communications. Chinese parents often tell children what they can buy and what they cannot buy. Parent-child communication patterns differ among parents of different demographic groups as well as age of children.

Parents with higher economic status engage more frequently in concept-oriented communication. Parents less often use socio-oriented communication when their children reach the age of 12. Parents allow older children to enjoy a greater autonomy in consumption and involve them more in family purchase decisions. Chinese parents seldom discuss commercials with children, and if they do, the discussions have little or no measurable influence on children's understanding of television advertising or children's attitudes toward television advertising. However, children are more likely to develop a positive attitude toward commercials if their parents often watch television with them. Therefore advertisers that target children need to develop good relationship with parents, too, so that the product category may become acceptable to parents. Overall, Chinese parents operate as relatively strict gatekeepers. They apparently want their kids to be practicing consumers in the sense of letting them make some buying decisions for themselves, but they guard what they buy and seldom involve them in purchases for the family. On the other hand they almost always seek the children's preferences before buying for them, thus, ceding to their children a lot of decision-making power.

Chapter 7

Parents' Attitudes toward Television Advertising and Children's Advertising

In the preceding chapter we discussed the demographic characteristics of Chinese parents, the parent-child communications about consumption, and family communications about television commercials. In this chapter, we are going to examine Chinese parents' attitudes toward television advertising in general and toward children's advertising in specific, and their control of their children's TV viewing. Also, we will look at how parents' attitudes toward advertising influence their children's attitudes toward advertising and the resulting implications for marketing to Chinese children.

In the next few sections, we are going to explore the following questions:

1. What are Chinese parents' attitudes toward television advertising in general, and specifically toward advertising that targets their children?
2. How do Chinese parents control children's viewing of television?
3. Do parents' attitudes toward advertising correlate with parental control of television viewing?
4. How do parents' attitudes toward advertising relate to their children's attitudes toward television commercials?

Chinese parents' attitudes toward advertising

Attitudes toward advertising in general have been studied primarily in North America and Europe (e.g. Alwitt and Prabhaker, 1992; Lutz, 1975; Mittal, 1994; Pollay and Mittal, 1993; Rossiter, 1977; Shavitt et al., 1998). Most of these studies are based on Bauer and Greyser's (1968) conceptualization of a two-dimensional measure of perceived economic and social effects of advertising such as encouraging materialism and manipulation of audiences. Also, concurrently, attitudes toward children's advertising have been studied on the two continents with particular concern for its persuasive influence on the children (e.g., Crosby and Grossbart, 1984; Robertson et al., 1989; Rose et al., 1998).

Recently, there have been studies of attitudes toward advertising in the Chinese societies. Several studies on attitudes of Chinese business executives in the late 80s and early 90s generally reported positive attitudes toward advertising (e.g. Kwan et al., 1983; Semenik et al., 1986). Public opinion studies of Chinese consumers, however, indicate there is a trend of increasing negative perceptions toward advertising. In a national probability sample survey conducted by China Central Television (CCTV) in 1987, three-quarters of the 24,900 respondents perceived television advertising as "essential" or "acceptable." In a survey of respondents in Beijing in the 1980s mass advertising was found to be the chief source of information about products among consumers (Zhao and Shen, 1995). Foreign advertisements appear to have the biggest impact among Chinese consumers, especially for those popular products that people can afford to buy or plan to buy. Further, it was found that Chinese consumers like creative, innovative, and lively advertisements. They are, however, very skeptical about advertisements using testimonials, as they think that actors are paid to say good things about the products (Zhao and Shen, 1995). Also, Chinese consumers are somewhat suspicious of advertised products because some of them still think that only bad products need to be advertised. This perception may be based on the fact that early advertisements often used exaggerated claims. Chinese consumers generally like foreign advertisements and find them appealing. This is probably because they have high regard for imported products from the West (Liang and Jacobs, 1994).

In another survey of 500 respondents in Beijing in 1996, consumers' overall attitude toward advertising in general was positive with about two-thirds of the sample considering advertising a good thing and half of the sample expressing liking of advertising (Chan, 1998). A more recent survey in 1999 of 583 young consumers ages 18 to 24 reflect mixed attitudes towards advertising (Liu, 2002). On the one hand, young consumers perceive advertising as essential to the prosperity of the economy and agree that advertising helps to raise the living standard.

On the other hand, they are annoyed by the deception and bias in advertising. They express a need for stronger regulation of advertisements. They believe that advertising influences children more than adults and agree that advertising aimed at children should be controlled (Liu, 2002). In a national survey of consumers' attitude toward advertising conducted by the China Consumer Association in 2000, over fifty percent of the 3,358 respondents held negative views about advertising of medicine, medical treatment and health products. Seventy-one percent of them perceived television advertisements as misleading and urged tighter control of advertisements by legal authorities (Modern Advertising, 2001). A survey of 2,953 consumers in 1995 found that attitudes toward advertising vary among different consumer lifestyle segments. Traditionalists and status quo consumers disapprove of advertising. Modern and generation X segments view advertising positively while transitioners reflect a more neutral attitude (Wei, 1997).

The Advertising Law enacted in February 1995 strictly governs advertising in all media in China. It does not provide for a limit on the amount of commercials per program hour on television. However, commercials are usually scheduled before or after a television program and seldom scheduled within programs. The national news at 7:00pm, one of the most popular programs in China, has attracted so many advertisers that it is common to have a commercial break of ten minutes running before it. Advertisers have to bid through auction for a precious five-second billboard commercial in order to appear in that particular commercial break. Advertising clutter is extremely severe due to the long duration of the commercial breaks and the abundance of very short commercials. Advertisers often use commercials 5–15 seconds in length. Table 7-1 shows a typical prime-time television schedule on CCTV-1 in May 2002. Between 18:46 and 22:07, or three hours and 21 minutes, there were 206 commercials aired. Due to this high degree of advertising clutter and the prevalence of irresponsible commercials that target Chinese audiences, we expect Chinese parents to hold negative attitudes toward television advertising.

Based on our conversations with parents in Beijing and newspaper articles about advertising in China, parents' main criticisms and praise of advertising can be summarized as done in Table 7-2. The list of

Table 7-1: A typical prime-time television schedule on CCTV-1 in May 2002

Time	Program/ commercial	Duration (minute: sec.)	No. of commercials	Average duration of commercial (sec.)
18:46–18:56	Commercials	9:35	57	10.1
18:56–19:00	Program preview	3:30		
19:00–19:33	National news	33:00		
19:33–19:34	Commercials	1:05	13	5.0
19:34–19:38	Weather forecast	3:40		
19:38–19:42	Commercials	3:30	14	15.0
19:42–19:58	Focus interview	16:15		
19:58–20:02	Commercials	4:10	15	16.7
20:02–20:02	Technology info	0:12		
20:02–20:02	Commercials	0:10	2	5.0
20:02–20:08	Technology info	6:30		
20:08–20:14	Commercials	5:55	28	12.7
20:14–21:00	Soap opera	46:00		
21:00–21:07	Commercials	6:35	31	12.7
21:07–21:27	Program	19:55		
21:27–21:33	Commercials	6:40	23	17.4
21:33–21:34	Program	1:00		
21:34–21:35	Commercials	0:34	6	5.7
21:35–22:02	Program	27:00		
22:02–22:07	Commercials	4:25	17	15.6
Total	TV programs	158:21 (79%)		
	Commercials*	42:39 (21%)	206	12.4

* Equivalent to about 14 minutes per hour.

criticisms makes it clear that parents are particularly concerned with advertising teaching their children bad habits and undesirable values. To the extent that parents have praise for advertising, it is for those ads that teach good habits and values.

In our survey on Chinese parents, apart from asking how parents communicate with children about consumption (as covered in the last chapter), we also measured parents' attitudes toward television advertising in general, and attitudes toward advertising that target their children in general. Attitudes toward television advertising in general are measured

Table 7-2: Chinese parents' criticism and praise of advertising

Criticism:
- Encouraging children to eat snacks with high sugar contents and therefore potentially harming their teeth
- Encouraging children to play with dangerous toys such as guns and knifes and with video games that contain violent activities
- Encouraging materialism which is in opposition to the Chinese tradition of frugality
- Encouraging children to conform thus discouraging their creativity
- Many advertisements are deceptive
- Inducing parent-child conflicts
- Using premiums to get children to buy the products and eventually lead to waste, as children are only interested in the premiums
- Teaching children inappropriate use of language by selectively changing wording in proverbs
- Using sounds and images that are scary to children
- Advertising of sensitive products including wine, female personal products and under garments.

Praise:
- Some advertisements are artistic and creative
- Some advertisements express warmth such as respect for elderly and caring for family members
- Some advertisements use national heroes that make you feel good about your country such as those featuring national athletes as spokespersons.
- Public services announcements are good for civic education. They crystallize complicated messages in a memorable slogan.

by a 7-item scale (Rossiter, 1977). The scale measures respondents' general skepticism toward television advertising (Boush et al., 1994), and their overall beliefs and reactions regarding advertising tactics. We ask parents to rate the seven items on a 5-point scale (1 = disagree strongly, 5 = agree strongly). After reverse coding selected items, means form the measure of attitude toward advertising with higher scores indicating more negative attitude toward advertising in general. Attitudes toward children's advertising were measured by asking respondents to rate on a 5-point scale over the seven items used by Crosby and Grossbart (1984) (1 = disagree strongly, 5 = agree strongly) and an additional statement about the influence of advertising on children's ability to think independently. After reverse coding selected items, the means form the measure of attitudes toward children's advertising with higher scores indicating more negative attitudes toward children's advertising. We expected the two scales to be similar. The data show a strong positive linear correlation between the two scales (r = 0.55), thus enhancing our confidence in the validity of the two measures. In other words, parents who dislike advertising in general also have negative attitudes toward children's advertising.

Parents' attitudes toward television advertising and children's advertising are summarized in Table 7-3. Statements are arranged in descending order of the mean values.

Chinese parents generally hold negative attitudes toward television advertising. They are skeptical about the truthfulness of television commercials. A large proportion of the parents believe that television commercials do not present a true picture of the product and do not tell the truth. Therefore over half do not believe the commercials. Though parents do not like most television commercials and consider them annoying, only about 37 percent perceive commercials as manipulative.

Chinese parents hold negative attitudes toward children's advertising too. Parents strongly feel that they have the responsibility to defend children from misleading commercials and over half support banning all television commercials during children's program hours. They are concerned about the bad influence of food advertising on children's eating habits. They generally are neutral about the amount of advertising directed at children and the possible family conflict brought by children's pestering. About half feel that advertising uses gimmicks to get their kids to buy products, but only 27 percent feel that advertising takes away children's independent thinking.

Chinese parents are dissatisfied with television advertising in general and children's advertising specifically. The dissatisfaction stems mainly from the perception that television advertising is biased and does not tell the truth. The current study gives evidence to the increasingly negative attitudes toward advertising among Chinese consumers.

Parents generally believe that food advertising to children encourages bad eating habits and they do not like promotional activities that target

Table 7-3: Parents' attitudes toward television advertising and
children's advertising

Items	Agree/ strongly agree (%)	Neutral (%)	Disagree/ Strongly disagree (%)	Overall mean	S.D.
Negative attitudes toward advertising				*3.6*	*0.5*
Television commercials tell only the good things about a product, they don't tell you the bad things.	81.5	7.5	11.0	4.0	1.0
Television commercials tell the truth. (R)	3.5	22.0	74.5	3.9	0.7
The products advertised the most on TV are always the best products to buy. (R)	7.8	27.5	64.7	3.7	0.8
We can believe what is said in commercials. (R)	8.2	36.1	55.7	3.6	0.8
I like most television commercials. (R)	11.0	35.5	53.5	3.5	0.9
Most television commercials are annoying.	51.1	32.2	16.7	3.5	1.0
Television commercials try to make people buy things they don't really need.	36.8	34.9	28.3	3.1	1.0
Negative attitudes toward children's advertising				*3.3*	*0.5*
Parents have the responsibility to explain the misleading contents in the advertisements to their children.	81.5	13.9	4.6	3.9	0.7
All advertising should be banned on children's program hours.	58.1	28.3	18.4	3.6	1.0
There is too much sugar in the foods advertised to children.	52.9	28.7	18.4	3.4	1.0
Advertising teaches children bad eating habits.	43.7	33.6	22.7	3.3	1.0
Advertisers use gimmicks such as lucky draw and premiums to get children to buy their products.	49.8	16.2	34.0	3.2	1.3
There isn't too much advertising directed at children. (R)	26.1	35.7	38.1	3.1	0.9
Advertising directed at children leads to family conflict.	36.9	34.4	28.7	3.1	1.0
Advertising makes children imitate and lose the ability to think independently.	26.8	42.0	31.2	2.9	1.0

R: reverse coded when compiling the mean.

their children. This echoes the generational difference in dietetic knowledge between the parents and the children. Parents believe that western snacks like chocolate are upsetting a balanced diet of hot and cold food (Guo, 2000). Marketers and advertisers should be aware that parents' negative attitudes toward advertising do have significant impact on their advertising activities. It is possible that negative attitudes toward advertising will eventually be translated into negative attitudes toward individual commercials or even advertised brands. These findings suggest that advertising agencies and advertisers should create more socially acceptable advertising messages. Parents' strong feeling that advertising should be banned during children's hours seems to suggest that Chinese parents rely on the government to set and enforce the rules to control the effects of advertising on children. This may be because parents do not perceive themselves having the knowledge or the ability to mediate the effects of advertising on children. As there is a lack of child-advocacy groups in China, dissatisfied parents can hardly express their concerns about children's advertising. To policy makers, the dissatisfaction with advertising may mean an urge for government regulation of deceptive commercials. If the regulatory body does not take the parents' concerns seriously, parents may develop a mistrust of the government. It could eventually undermine the credibility of the government.

Similar to family communication patterns, parental attitudes toward television advertising and children's advertising vary with demographic characteristics of parents and children. Negative attitudes toward television advertising and negative attitudes toward children's advertising are strongest among parents of high economic status (high educational level, high household income, and among teachers and researchers). These groups of parents are more critical and are more concerned about the deceptive contents of advertising. Parents of younger children are more critical about children's advertising than parents of older children. Parents of younger children ages 6-7 worry more that children may lose the ability to think independently than parents of older children. Parents of young children ages 6-7 worry more that advertising directed at children will lead to family conflicts than parents of older children. Parents of older children worry less about this, probably because older children use other persuasive strategies than mere pestering. Generally, mothers have a more negative attitude toward children's advertising than fathers. Mothers are more concerned than fathers about the sugar content in snacks. They also worry more that children will lose their ability to think independently. Mothers also are more likely than fathers to perceive that they have the responsibility to explain misleading advertising contents in the advertisements to their children.

How do parents control children's television viewing?

Previous studies indicate that Chinese parents exert great control over children's use of mass media. In a study of 529 grade 6 and grade 10 students in Beijing, 74 percent of young children said there are rules at home regarding how long they can watch TV (Greenberg et al., 1991). The most common forms of media mediation for television are familiarization with types of programs children watch and co-viewing with children. Parents of younger children more often tell them not to watch certain programs and recommend programs for them to watch. Children report that parents sometimes use television time as a potential reward or punishment. In a survey of 176 parents in Beijing and Jiaozuo, over 85 percent of parents demonstrate control over viewing time as well as contents (Zhao, 1996). The purpose of parental control over viewing time was to minimize the chance of children being distracted from their studies by television. One typical rule was that viewing was allowed only after children finished their homework. Most parents mentioned that they encourage their children to watch intellectual and morally uplifting television programs while prohibiting them from viewing programs with love and sexual contents. This tight parental control reflects Chinese parents' concern with the breakdown of conventional moral standards and norms under the challenge of an increasingly commercialized mass media culture (Zhao, 1996). In our focus group study with parents in Beijing in 2001, some parents reported that they never allow their children to watch commercials about underwear or female personal products. Parents reported that they were afraid that these commercials would trigger children's interest in sex and love. When these commercials are on, they either will switch channels or ask their children to excuse themselves for a while.

In our survey among parents, we asked them whether they place any restriction on children's TV viewing. Parents could choose either "no restriction" or "yes, there is restriction." Parents answering the latter one were asked to choose the type of restrictions including "no TV at all," "restriction on which programs the child can watch," "restriction on when the child can watch," "restriction on how many hours each day the child can watch," and an open-ended answer of other restrictions.

Parents could select more than one type of restriction. We also ask parents to what extent they agree with the statement, "parents have influence on children's attitude toward television advertising" on a 5-point scale (1 = disagree strongly, 5 = agree strongly). This statement was intended to measure perceived parental influence on children's attitudes toward TV viewing.

Table 7-4 summarizes the extent to which Chinese parents' control television viewing. Its shows that ninety-eight percent of parents report exercising at least one measure to control children's television viewing. The most common types of control include restricting the contents and amount of time of viewing. Three percent of parents do not allow their children to watch any television. Fifty percent of parents agree or strongly agree that they have influence on their children's attitude toward television advertising, while one third neither agree nor disagree. One-sixth of parents disagrees or strongly disagrees that they have influence on their children's attitude toward television advertising.

Parental control of television viewing does not differ among demographic characteristics of parents and children. In Chapter 6, we reported that older children enjoy a greater autonomy in consumption. Our survey of parents indicates that parental control of television viewing does not diminish even when their children get older. Parental control of Chinese children's TV viewing time is stricter than the control over their spending.

Compared to Greenberg et al.'s (1991) data and Zhao's (1996) data collected in the 80s, parents now report even stronger control of their children's television viewing. Zhao (1996) argues that parental control over media content reflects an ever more competitive school system and the increasing commercialization of television. If so, the current finding suggests that the school system has become even more competitive and/ or television contents are more commercialized than in the past ten to fifteen years. Parental control exists in both content and time of watching. This probably reflects Chinese parents concern about what their children watch as well as how much they watch. Parents are now stepping in to replace the Party to screen the flow of undesirable ideologies and values to their children. To marketers and advertisers, this is important because their commercials must be scheduled near television programs or time

Table 7-4: Parental control of television viewing

Control TV Viewing	%
No control	2.5
Yes, there is control*:	97.5
– Place restriction on which programs my child can watch	57.8
– Place restriction on when my child can watch	45.7
– Place restriction on how many hours each day my child can watch	27.5
– Watch on weekends only	3.5
– No TV	3.0
– Watch after finishing homework	2.9

* For those parents who have controlled, he or she could choose more than one type of control, e.g., 57.8% of all the parents sampled place restriction on which programs the child can watch.

periods that are acceptable to the parents. Otherwise, the children will never have a chance to see these commercials. As parental control occurs in all walks of life, the single child policy has now defined a new relationship between parents and their only child. The close monitoring of children's viewing behavior occurs in parents of all demographic strata irrespective of age and sex of children.

Correlation between parents' attitude toward advertising and parental mediation

As the level of parental control of television viewing of children is already very high (98 percent of families with some control), it is not positively correlated with parents' attitudes toward television advertising or with attitude toward children's advertising. It suggests that parents cannot tighten the control of watching even if they hold more negative attitudes. Discussion with children about commercials is correlated with parents' attitude toward television advertising. Parents who hold more negative attitude toward television advertising actually hold less discussion with their children about commercials. So, if parents do not like commercials, they tend not to talk about them with children. Parents who are critical of advertising are not participating actively to mediate the effects of television advertising on children by providing on-the-spot guidance to children. From a consumer education point of view, the finding is worrisome.

Parents who have a more negative attitude toward television advertising perceive that they have a greater influence on their children's attitudes, despite the fact that they seldom discuss commercials with them. It suggests that Chinese parents perceive that they can exercise their influence through coercion, rather than through family communication. The following section will examine whether perceived parental influence matches with actual influence on children.

Parental influence on children's attitude toward television advertising

In the previous chapter, we found that parental discussion with children about commercials has no impact on children's understanding of television advertising. But, does parents' attitude toward television advertising have any impact on children's attitude toward television advertising?

We compiled Pearson correlations between parents' attitude toward television advertising and children's liking and perceived truthfulness of television commercials. Firstly, we found that parents' attitude toward television advertising is mildly correlated with children's liking of television commercials ($r = 0.07$, $p < 0.01$). Children whose parents hold a more negative attitude toward television advertising dislike commercials more. Secondly, we found that parents' attitude toward television advertising is correlated with children's perceived truthfulness of television commercials ($r = 0.07$, $p < 0.05$). Children whose parents hold a more negative attitude toward television advertising put less trust in commercials. Thirdly, we found that the correlation between parents' attitude toward television advertising and children's attitude toward television advertising is more profound for older children than for younger children. For example, the correlation between parents' attitude toward television advertising and children's liking of commercials was not significant for children in the age groups 6–7 and 8–9. For children aged 10–11, the correlation was 0.17 ($p < 0.001$) and for children aged 12–14, the correlation was 0.18 ($p < 0.001$). One may expect that parental influence will be higher for younger children. The results show just the opposite. We think that this may be because younger children are more egocentric and do not pay much attention to what their parents think about advertising. Older children, however, are able to adopt a dual perspective of their own as well as that of their parents. They are therefore more subjected to parental influence.

Finally, we found that perceived parental influence is not related with children's liking or children's trust of television commercials. In other words, children's attitude toward television advertising does not differ among those parents who perceive they have strong influence on children and those who perceive they don't have strong influence.

Some conclusions

Chinese parents hold negative attitudes toward both television advertising and children's advertising. The negative attitude originates mainly from the perception that advertising is deceptive and annoying. Parents exercise tight control over children's television viewing. They perceive that they have great influence on children's attitudes toward advertising even though they seldom discuss television commercials with their children. Older children's attitude toward commercials reflects largely their parents' attitude toward television advertising while younger children's attitude toward commercials does not.

Results from this chapter and the previous one indicate that parents could have significant impact on children's perception of consumption and television advertising through family communication and mediation of television viewing. Therefore, when marketing to children in China, advertisers must pay attention to the influence of their parents. Products that parents may not like should consider an advertising medium other than television to reach children. Marketers who target children should present their messages in a credible manner in order to gain trust from parents and children. In view of the high parental control of television viewing and parents' negative attitudes toward television advertising to children, advertisers should consider using outdoor media, point-of-purchase promotion, event marketing, and Internet advertising. Also, it is suggested that the advertising industry in general promote itself and its beneficial features to parents.

Chapter 8

Content Analysis of Television Commercials Targeted to Chinese Children

In Chapter 2 television was shown to be the most important source of product information for Chinese children. They give it more votes as the preferred source of information for new products than parents and peers combined. This is in spite of China being a collective society that relies heavily on family and friends for guidance in decision-making including purchase decision-making. Of course, the major portion of the product information that children seek comes from advertising during television programming. (The other significant source of information is from the television programs themselves.) Because of television's heightened importance in the lives of Chinese children we devoted the past several chapters to examining in some detail the attitudes that Chinese children and their parents hold about television advertising. In this chapter we want to give a great deal of consideration to the ads themselves, that is, to empirically examining actual television commercials that are intended for children. As an aid to understanding the analysis, we will do some comparing with their counterparts in the United States. Perhaps, then, the reader can gain a better appreciation for the feelings that the Chinese children and their parents hold toward television advertising.

Background: A glance at children's television today

CCTV is the largest and the most influential TV station in China. It has 13 channels (including a 24-hour news channel that began a trial operation in May 2003) and broadcast over 240 hours a day. About three-quarters of the programs are locally produced (CCTV web site, 2002). According to a study in 1996, children's programs made up 7 percent of total daily programs of 120 hours in all CCTV channels (Chinese Academy of Social Sciences, 2000). Local TV channels and satellite channels also carried children's TV programs. Popular children's TV programs include:

- "The Big Windmill" (*da feng che*): broadcast on CCTV-1 and CCTV-7, is a variety-show program with a great deal of information. The program was introduced in June 1995. The target audiences are children ages 3–12. The program has four components: animation, pre-school children's program, short series, and TV film. The program has blended ideological content, knowledge and entertainment. The rating for children aged 4–14 is among one of the highest (CVSC-TNS Research, 2002).

- "Cartoon City" (*dong hua cheng*): broadcast on CCTV-1 and CCTV-7, consists of nationally produced cartoons. The target audiences are children ages 3–12. The particular cartoon broadcast in October 2002 was "Journey to the West."

- "Sesame, Open the Door" (*zhi ma kai men*): broadcast on CCTV-1 and CCTV-7, is an educational program for elementary school children. The program features scientific knowledge of daily life, for example, the water supply system in a household.

- "The Colorful World" (*qi se guang*): broadcast on Beijing TV Station. This is a children's variety show with the highest rating of 12 percent among children ages 4–14 in Beijing (CVSC-TNS Research, 2002).

- "The Second Starting Line" (*di er qi pao xian*): broadcast on CCTV-1 and CCTV-7. The targets are secondary school students. The program is divided into two parts. The first part is a talk show while the second part features overseas and home made videos about the lives of secondary school students in China.

Children's TV ratings start to pick up at 5:30 pm and drop significantly after 10:00pm (CVSC-TNS Research, 2002). Table 8-1 displays a typical television schedule of children's after-school programming on CCTV-1 in May 2002. Essentially it reveals that for a period of an hour and a half there are continuous cartoons and variety shows for kids interspersed with many commercials. The table shows also that approximately 83 percent of the time period is filled with

Table 8-1: A typical television schedule of children's program on CCTV-1 in May 2002

Time	Program/ Commercial	Duration (min: sec.)	No. of commer- cials	Commercials target at adults	Commercials target at children	Average duration of commercial (sec.)
17:28:00-17:29:30	TV guide	0:30				
17:29:30-17:30:00	Commercials	0:30	6	5	1	5.0
17:30:00-17:45:35	Cartoon City	15:35				
17:45:35-17:46:20	Commercials	0:45	2	0	2	22.5
17:46:20-17:56:57	Cartoon City	10:37				
17:56:57-17:57:40	Commercials	0:43	2	0	2	21.5
17:57:40-18:00:00	Cartoon City	2:20				
18:00:00-18:05:00	News in brief	5:00				
18:05:00-18:07:20	Commercials	1:40	9	1	8	11.1
18:07:20-18:19:06	Big Windmill	11:46				
18:19:06-18:19:36	Commercials	0:30	2	0	2	15.0
18:19:36-18:32:32	Big Windmill	12:56				
18:32:32-18:33:02	Commercials	0:30	2	0	2	15.0
18:33:02-18:44:40	Big Windmill	11:38				
18:44:40-18:45:53	Commercials	1:13	4	0	4	18.3
18:45:53-18:46:53	Big Windmill	0:42				
18:46:35-18:56:05	Commercials	9:30	58	54	4	9.8
18:56:05-19:00:00	National anthem & TV guide	3:30				
Total	TV programs 76:39 (83%)					
	Commercials* 15:21 (17%)		85	60 (71%)	25 (29%)	10.8

* Equivalent to about 10 minutes per hour.

programming and 17 percent with ads. A closer look at the ads reveals that there are 85 of them with an average length of around 11 seconds. Thus, there are a relatively large number of commercials made possible by each being presented in a short period of time, usually from 5 to 10 seconds each. Presenting ads in short bursts such as this probably makes the ad messages easier for the children to comprehend and absorb. If one compared this 90 minutes of afternoon programming for Chinese children with its counterpart in the United States, for example, one would notice a sharp difference. There would be only half the number of ads targeted to U.S. children, and each would be approximately twice as long, or around 20–25 seconds. On the other hand, afternoon programming for children in the U.S. is around 180 minutes, or twice as long as that of China TV.

There is another substantive difference in the ads positioned before and after the children's programs in China and those in the United States. Almost three-fourths (71 percent) of the ads in China are targeted to adults, although the children surely receive them and process them since they are adjacent to their programs. Only 29 percent of the ads seem to be targeted to kids. In the U.S. this percent would be close to 100 percent, that is, practically all products advertised on children's programming would be intended for kids.

We can make a closer examination of these ads on Chinese children's TV programming by looking at Table 8-2. This table totals and classifies the ads for a week on CCTV-1's afternoon programming for kids. When tallied for a week we find that the greatest share of ads on kids' programming, 66 percent, 377 ads, are for adults, while 34 percent, or 194 ads, are intended specifically for children. Table 8-2 shows the wide variety of products advertised to adults during children's programming, for example, medicines, home furnishings and furniture. Clearly these are not products for kids even though they are presented with kids programming. We do not know if the advertisers intend these ads to be seen by children or even to be positioned with children's programs. But this is not unusual in China. For example, we looked at afternoon children's programming in Beijing, Chengdu and Nanjing. In Beijing the percent of ads for adults was 55 percent, in Chengdu this percent was 50, while in Nanjing it was nearly zero. We should note that there are some products generally classified as adult products that are also shared with children, for example, toothpaste and shampoo. In these cases, it may not be unexpected that marketers of these items would target children on television programming in order to encourage the children to ask their parents for certain brands of the products.

Going back to Table 8-2 and looking at just the ads targeted to kids — that present products normally intended for children — we see that around 90 percent are intended to satisfy tastes and appetites — foods, confections, and beverages such as milk, jelly, bubble gum, and noodles — while the remainder are mainly about play. Comparing these categories with those advertised to kids in the West, we would find around half food and half play items for Western kids.

To get a better understanding of TV commercials that target Chinese

Table 8-2: **Types of products and number of commercials presented in a week of children's programming on CCTV-1**

Mainly for adults	
Product category	No. of commercials
OTC medicines	76
Air conditioners	70
Furniture and household durables	53
Corporate ads and business services	33
Automobiles	31
Public service announcements (PSAs)	26
Household products	23
Clothing	20
Cold cure and cough syrup	15
Mobile phones	12
Credit cards	7
Personal items	6
Pharmaceutical companies	5
Total	377

Mainly for children	
Product category	No. of commercials
Milk and milk powder	53
Jelly	38
Growth vitamins	34
Biscuits	20
Beverages	13
Ham and sausage	11
Noodle	7
Bubble gums	7
Tonics	6
Theme parks	4
Ice cream	1
Total	194

children, we will present a study that content analyzes all the ads for a long period of time that focus only on China's kids — eliminating those that present adult products. In order to have a greater understanding of these ads, they will be compared in detail with a similar group of ads for U.S. kids.

Background of the study

This study carefully describes the content of Chinese children's commercials, compares them with commercials targeted to American children, examines them for differences, and attempts to delineate the underlying reasons for the differences (McNeal and Ji, 1998; Ji and McNeal, 2001). According to communication theory, communication content, such as TV advertising, is the consequence of antecedent conditions or contextual factors including cultural, social, and economic ones that have led to or shaped its construction (Riffe, Lacy, and Fico, 1998). A basic premise of this study is that children's commercials are a reflection of cultural, social, and economic conditions where the commercials are developed and broadcast. Therefore, differences between Chinese and U.S. children's commercials can be explained by differences in these three dimensions between the two countries. Hypotheses are proposed regarding how the content of children's commercials might be expected to differ between the two countries as a result of each antecedent condition. To test the hypotheses, researchers simultaneously video taped and analyzed children's commercials in the two countries periodically for 18 months.

Cultural factors

Numerous studies have shown that advertising is a reflection of the culture and philosophies. From the viewpoint of Geert Hofstede (1994, p. 4), a noted Dutch social scientist, a nation's culture is defined as "collective programming of the mind which distinguishes the members of one group or category of people from those of another." Through a 40-country survey, Hofstede identified four dimensions of culture that he termed: power distance, uncertainty avoidance, individualism, and masculinity. A fifth dimension, Confucian dynamism, or long-term versus short-term orientation, surfaced in a separate study. These five dimensions are used here to compare the cultural differences between the U.S. and China. For each, the differences between the two nations are discussed mainly from the viewpoint of Hofstede, and then hypotheses are proposed regarding the content of children's television advertising in each.

Table 8-3: Results and hypothesis testing of content analysis of Chinese and U.S. children's commercials

	China (%) N = 132	U.S. (%) N = 299	Chi-square statistics	p	Supported (food commercials only)
H1a: Adult spokesperson/ character	18.9	37.1	22.8	<0.001	No (no)
H1b: Adult voice-over	62.9	75.5	5.7	<0.05	No (no)
H2: Showing product in use	74.2	78.3	2.0	n.s.	No (yes)
H3: Informational content					Yes (yes)
– Quality	25.8	2.7	55.5	<0.001	
– Texture	14.4	1.0	33.9	<0.001	
H4a: Fun/happiness Appeal	14.4	43.5	32.3	<0.001	Yes (yes)
H4b: Adventure appeal	3.0	14.7	12.6	<0.001	Yes (yes)
H5a: Males as models	67.4	52.5	8.3	<0.01	Yes (yes)
H5b: Males as spokesperson	28.8	11.0	21.0	<0.001	Yes (yes)
H5c: Males used in voice-overs	24.2	10.0	15.0	<0.001	Yes (yes)
H6a: Popularity appeal	12.1	4.0	9.9	<0.01	Yes (yes)
H6b: Uniqueness appeal	14.1	12.4	0.3	n.s.	No (yes)
H7: Product benefit appeal					Yes (yes)
– Effectiveness	0.0	0.0	NA	NA	
– Health	38.6	7.0	65.8	<0.001	
– Economy	3.8	3.7	NA	NA	
– Convenience	6.1	2.0	4.8	<0.05	
H8a: Scholastic activities	1.5	1.6	NA	NA	No (no)
H8b: Athletic activities	2.3	2.0	NA	NA	No (no)
H9: Ethnic groups	GP	GP	GP	GP	Yes (yes)

NA: Chi-square test is not applicable because the cell size is too small.
GP: More than one group is involved in the result.

Power distance

Power distance refers to the extent to which less powerful members of organizations and institutions (like the family) accept and expect that power is distributed unequally. Power distance is a social norm that originates in early socialization by the family, the school, and other institutions of society. It is reflected in the values of both the less powerful and more powerful members of society and it influences the way people accept and give authority. China has a long history of being an authoritarian society, which emphasizes Confucius' five cardinal relations between sovereign and minister, father and son, husband and wife, old and young, and friends. Compared to Americans who have low power distance, Chinese have a stronger respect for authority and are prone to accept authority without question. Therefore, it comes natural for young people to accept authority from opinion leaders, including older people and family elders who recommend products/services in commercials. This authority tradition in China leads to the following two hypotheses:

H1a: A higher percent of Chinese children's commercials has adults as spokes-person/characters — authorities to children — than those of the United States.

H1b: A higher percent of Chinese children's commercials has adult voice-overs than those of the United States.

Uncertainty avoidance

A second dimension of national culture, called uncertainty avoidance, focuses on how societies deal with unknown aspects of the future. Compared to the United States, China has a high index of uncertainty avoidance. One characteristic of a high uncertainty avoidance culture is that it has little tolerance for ambiguity in one's perceptions. In the case of advertising to children, it is logical to assume that compared to U.S. children, Chinese counterparts have less tolerance for ambiguity in advertising. In order to reduce the ambiguity, advertisers in China may tend to focus more on demonstration by showing products in use, thus emphasizing concrete, functional, and utilitarian product benefits. Therefore,

H2: A higher percent of Chinese children's commercials shows products in use than those in the United States.

Chinese's low tolerance for ambiguity may also imply that they have great need for information about an advertised product. Some recent work by one of the authors that has been noted in previous chapters suggests that Chinese children utilize a wide range of sources to learn about new products and rank TV the most important information source of all (McNeal and Ji, 1999). Given the strong tendency of Chinese children to expect new product information from TV, marketers in China are more likely to include it in the commercials to children.

Thus, it is hypothesized that,

H3: A higher percent of Chinese children's commercials contains informational content than those of the United States.

Individualism

This dimension of national culture describes the relationship between the individual and the collectivity that prevails in a given society and is intimately linked with societal norms. A commonly shared societal norm in collectivist cultures is to place collective goals ahead of personal goals where there is a conflict between the two. One of the connotations of high individualism is the extensive appeal of enjoyment and pleasure in life. Compared to collectivist societies, individualistic societies place higher emphasis on individual variety and pleasure. A recent empirical study by Zhang and Gelb (1996) suggests that Chinese consumers respond more favorably to a collectivistic than to an individualistic appeal. Therefore, compared to the children's commercials in the United States, those of Chinese are less likely to portray an advertised product's individualistic appeals such as fun/happiness or adventure. Thus,

H4a: A lesser percent of Chinese children's commercials emphasizes the fun/happiness appeal of the advertised product than those of the United States.

H4b: A lesser percent of Chinese children's commercials emphasizes the adventure appeal of the advertised product than those of the United States.

Masculinity

A fourth dimension is defined as the degree to which a society is characterized by masculinity (assertiveness) versus femininity (nurturance). The issue of the duality of the sexes is whether biological differences between the sexes should or should not have implications for their roles in social activity. China is a traditionally male-dominant society and Chinese parents prefer to have boys rather than girls. Male children carry on the family name, inherit the family property, and play a special role in family traditions. The U.S. scores moderately high on the index of masculinity where studies have consistently revealed that TV advertising aimed at children in the U.S. features more boys than girls. Although a direct comparison of the degree of masculinity between China and U.S. is not available, Williams and Best (1990), in a series of studies involving 24 countries, suggested that, in general, lower levels of urbanization and education were associated with adherence to more traditional gender roles. Compared to the United States, China has a much lower level of urbanization and education, so China may be assumed to have a higher level of masculinity. This assumption was confirmed somewhat by a study by Cheng (1997a) which revealed that advertising in both China and the U.S. portrays more men in occupational roles and more women in non-occupational ones, but Chinese television advertising reinforces this stereotype more than its U.S. counterpart. Thus it is hypothesized that

H5a: A higher percent of Chinese children's commercials uses males as models than those of the United States.

H5b: A higher percent of Chinese children's commercials uses males as spokespersons than those of the United States.

H5c: A higher percent of Chinese children's commercials uses males as voice-overs than those of the United States.

Confucian dynamism

On the "dynamic" side of this dimension one finds values oriented towards the future, like thrift (saving) and perseverance. On the opposite side one finds values oriented towards the past and present, such as reciprocation, face, and tradition. Face is defined by Ho (1976, p. 867) as follows, "Face is lost when the individual, either through his action or that of people closely related to him, fails to meet essential requirements placed upon him by virtue of the social position he occupies." The concept of face is much more pervasive in Chinese culture than it is in the United States. One type of face is called *lian*. A person with *lian* has high status by fulfilling a role and following appropriate standards of behavior. It should be noted that this dimension is not totally unrelated to the collectivism dimension. In fact, many Asian countries, including China, score high on both dimensions. However, the collectivism/individualism dimension deals primarily with how to prioritize personal and collective goals. Face saving, one facet of Confucian dynamism, deals more with how much a person is concerned about looking right to others. Here, we suggest that a Chinese commercial is unlikely to emphasize the uniqueness of a product that does not follow well-accepted standards because the usage may result in people losing face. Therefore, because of this difference in Confucian dynamism (saving face) from the U.S., Chinese children's commercials are more likely to emphasize a product's universal recognition and acceptance by consumers but not its unparalleled nature, or what might be termed, popularity and uniqueness, respectively. Using these same terms, it is hypothesized that,

H6a: A higher percent of Chinese children's commercials tends to emphasize the popularity value of an advertised product than those of the United States.

H6b: A lower percent of Chinese children's commercials tends to emphasize the uniqueness value of an advertised product than those of the United States.

Hofstede demonstrated that the variation across countries among his four national cultural dimensions is associated with variation in a number of other national indices. For example, the power distance scores for different countries are negatively related to their economic wealth and latitude and positively related to their population size and population growth rates, while individualism scores are positively related to economic wealth and latitude and negatively related to population growth rate. However, there are still some economic and social differences that are not reflected adequately by the national culture, but by economic development.

Economic development

The development of advertising in the U.S. can be divided into four stages: product information, product image, personalization, and lifestyle that encompassed seven decades from the 1910s to the 1980s (Leiss, Kline, and Jhally, 1990). China experienced its first advertising boom in the 1920s and 1930s, but its development came to a halt when the Chinese Communist Party began to institute a centrally planned economy after 1949. Commercial advertising did not return until the late 1970s when China embarked on its market-oriented economic reform movement. Although the growth of the advertising industry in China was very rapid between 1981 and 1995, it is still in its early development stage, which primarily emphasizes the product itself, explaining its benefits and uses. Given the relatively short history of China modern advertising industry, it is hypothesized that:

H7: A higher percent of Chinese children's commercials emphasizes product benefits and use (quality, effectiveness, health, economy, or convenience) than those of the United States.

Social factors

China's one-child policy has been fundamentally in place in its urban population since the early 1980s. Consequently, the single child receives most of the love and attention of both parents as well as those of four grandparents, and this is apparent in the marketplace in various ways. Today nearly 40% of a typical family's income, or around US$90 each month, is spent on its children. These expenses are often regarded as an investment by parents who want their only child to become healthy and wise. The emphasis on children's health is highly related to the importance of children being able to receive a good education, which is considered the most important path to success in China. Parents in urban China spend a large proportion of their family income on such things as special schools, tutors, computers, piano lessons, and other extracurricular activities for their kids. On the other hand, U.S. children and their parents give strong emphasis to athletic activities and accomplishments. Research into magazine and television advertisements has showed that young people in the U.S. are depicted in athletic activities more than in scholarly activities. Therefore, it is hypothesized that

H8a: A higher percent of Chinese children's commercials portrays scholastic activities than those of the United States.

H8b: A lower percent of Chinese children's commercials portrays athletic/exercise activities than those of the United States.

Another social factor that may influence advertising is ethnicity. In total there are 56 different races in China. The largest one, Han, constitutes more than 84% of the total population. Since most of the minorities live in the rural and relatively poor areas, their spending power is very limited and they are widely ignored by marketers' targeting efforts. Although White is the dominant ethnic group in the United States, Black, Hispanic, Asian and other groups are growing rapidly and are projected to constitute nearly 30% of the total population by 2005 according to the U.S. Bureau of the Census. Recently, U.S. marketers began to recognize the economic power of minority groups and as a result target them more intensively including using more TV advertising. This ethnic difference leads to the following hypothesis:

H9: A lower percent of Chinese children's commercials includes minority models than those of the United States.

In all, 15 hypotheses are tested to determine if differences or similarities in children's commercials are a reflection of cultural, social, and economic differences between the two countries. Concurrently, a more in-depth understanding of advertising to children in China should emerge.

A content analysis study of children's commercials

Content analysis has been the tool of choice for analyzing communications for many years and it is the standard analytical tool for advertising studies. Thus, content analysis was used in this study to classify content of the commercials. Children's TV commercials were recorded simultaneously in the U.S. and China during an 18-month period (1998–

1999) and then content analyzed. For more details about the research methodology, please refer to Appendix 8-1.

The unit of analysis was each complete television commercial targeted to children. Two criteria defined a children-targeted commercial in China and the U.S.: (1) the product shown in a commercial is commonly consumed by children age 12 and under; and (2) the commercial itself is developed for children as the primary audience. The first criterion was met by choosing commercials that presented products clearly suitable for the consumption by children and unlikely to be consumed by teenagers and adults. The second criterion was met by choosing commercials that appeared before, during, and right after children programming. This definition also embraces public service announcements (PSAs) which are usually classified as advertisements for social products, such as environmental protection and health, and are typically paid for in both the U.S. and China. Program promos (65 from U.S. and 20 from China), however, were excluded from the analysis since they do not focus on either commercial or social products. In addition, duplicate commercials were excluded from the sample in order to eliminate redundancies that might skew the results. A net total of 431 television commercials — 299 from the United States and 132 from China — were obtained during the four weeks of the study. Specifically, 30.1% of U.S. commercials appeared on Nickelodeon, 27.1% appeared on WB Kids, 24.1% appeared on FOX, and 18.7% appeared on ABC. As for commercials recorded in China, 37.1% of them appeared on CCTV1, 24.2% appeared on BCTV Cable 1, 22.0% appeared on CCTV2, 9.1% appeared on Beijing TV-1, 7.6% appeared on Beijing TV-2.

Findings

Of all the products advertised in Chinese children's commercials during the research period, 81.8 percent of them are food products, mainly dairy items, noodles, soft drinks, salty chips, and gelatin products — very similar to the nearly 90 percent shown in Table 8-2. This percentage is a much lower 30.8 percent for U.S. counterparts. The largest group of products advertised in U.S. children's commercials is toys (55.5 percent).

The food dominance of Chinese ads and the toy dominance of U.S. ads perhaps summarize the different priorities of need gratification between the two countries. In China, feeding children healthy and well is considered a high priority given its long history of starvation during two thirds of this century. In the U.S., on the other hand, providing children good food is a given, so the focus tends to be on satisfying their higher order needs of play and entertainment. Even among U.S. food ads such as McDonald's meals, General Mills cereals, and Oreo cookies, the emphasis is on fun and happiness. Other products that are common in the two sets of ads are: social products (7.7 percent for the U.S. and 2.3 percent for China), motion pictures (2.3 percent for both the U.S. and China), books, and music (1.0 percent for the U.S. and 3.8 percent for China). There are four ads for retail stores in the U.S. group; two in China. Also, there are three ads in China for medicines while there are none for this category in the U.S. Interestingly, books and music are not heavily advertised in either country although education through consumption is urged in both. Educational toys for children, for example, are experiencing strong demand in the U.S., while books for children are very popular retailed items in China.

There is a difference in the nature of the brands advertised between the two countries. It appears that Chinese children are increasingly exposed to Western brands, mainly from the United States, although domestic brands still constitute a majority of the products advertised. In China, eight of 132 commercials contain brands from the U.S. (KFC, McDonald's, Oreo cookies, Tang beverage, Safeguard soap, Disney CDs, Kraft ice cream, Pepsi), one from Singapore (Wei Ta hot cereal), and one from Japan (Audi toy model). U.S. children, on the other hand, are mainly surrounded by U.S. brands. There is also some overlapping in advertised brands: KFC meals, McDonald's meals, and Oreo cookies appeared in both samples, which presumably reflects a global targeting effort by these international companies since the ads were gathered at the same time.

There are also length differences in the TV commercials between the two nations. A small percent (5.3) of Chinese children's commercials was five seconds long. There were actually no five-second commercials among the U.S. ads. Fifteen-second commercials constituted 54.5 percent of Chinese children's commercials. This percent was 31.8 percent for those of the United States. The majority (67.2 percent) of U.S. children's commercials were 30 seconds long. On average, a Chinese children's commercial is 20.7 seconds while the length of a U.S. commercial is 25.5 seconds.

A summary of the hypotheses testing is presented in Table 8-3 and shows that of the 15 proposed hypotheses, nine are supported by the data in the sample, while six, H1a & b, H2, H6b and H8a & b, are not. The following section will report the findings and hypothesis testing in detail. An examination of the sample suggests that while the range of product categories advertised is about the same in both countries, the predominance of food commercials in China (81.8 percent) may confound the explanatory power of cultural, social, and economic differences in commercial differences. In order to solve this problem, food commercials from China and the U.S. are compared to determine if controlling for product category in the analysis would change the conclusions about hypothesis testing. Ideally, the analyses should control all the product categories and compare the commercial content within the same product category between the two countries. The small percentage of non-food commercials in China, however, limits this possibility. Therefore, only the food commercials from the two countries are compared as a proxy for controlling product category. The testing of the hypotheses using only food data are reported in parentheses in the last column of Table 8-3. The result suggests that when only food commercials are analyzed, H2 and H7b are found to be supported in addition to those that are supported by comparing the commercials of all the product categories.

Cultural factors

❏ *Power distance*

Since China has a higher level of power distance than the United States, it was expected that a higher percent of Chinese children's commercials would have adults as spokespersons/characters (H1a) and voice-overs (H1b) than those of the United States. The result, however, shows the opposite scenario. U.S. children's commercials are more likely to use adult spokes persons/characters (37.1 percent vs. 18.9 percent) and more adult voice-overs (75.5 percent vs. 62.9 percent) than those of Chinese. Therefore, H1a and H1b are not supported. These hypotheses are not supported even after controlling the product categories presented in the commercials from the two countries.

❑ *Uncertainty avoidance*

Given the high uncertainty avoidance tendency of Chinese consumers, it was expected that Chinese children's commercials would more likely show products in use to reduce any ambiguity (H2). The data disconfirm this hypothesis. The percentage of children commercials that show products in use is 74.2 percent for China and 78.3 percent for the United States. However, when only food commercials from the two countries are compared, H2 gains support. That is, Chinese children's food commercials are more likely to show the product in use than those of the United States (71.8 percent vs. 57.4 percent).

It was also anticipated that Chinese children's commercials would more likely include useful information content to avoid ambiguity. The results show that Chinese children's commercials are more likely than those of the U.S. to include two kinds of useful information about the advertised products: product texture (14.4 percent vs. 1.0 percent) and product quality (25.8 percent vs. 2.7 percent). Thus, H3 is supported.

❑ *Individualism*

All the hypotheses (H4a-b) about the impact of individualism on commercials received support. Chinese children's commercials are less likely to portray the fun/happiness appeal (14.4 percent vs. 43.5 percent) and adventure appeal (3.0 percent vs. 14.7 percent) than those of the United States.

❑ *Masculinity*

It was hypothesized that compared to U.S. children's commercials, a higher percent of Chinese children's commercials would choose males as models (H5a), spokespersons (H5b), and voice-overs (H5c). All three are supported as shown in Table 8-3. In the Chinese commercials, a higher percent of males serve as models (67.4 percent vs. 52.5 percent), spokespersons (28.8 percent vs. 11.0 percent), and voice-overs (24.2 percent vs. 10.0 percent) than in those in the United States.

❏ *Confucian dynamism*

The hypotheses about the impact of Confucian dynamism on commercial messages received mixed results. Consistent with our expectations, Chinese children's commercials are more likely to emphasize the popularity appeal than those of the U.S. (12.1 percent vs. 4.0 percent). It was expected that a lower percent of Chinese children's commercials would emphasize the uniqueness appeal. When all the commercials from the two countries were analyzed, little difference was found between them in portraying the uniqueness appeal (14.1 percent vs. 12.4 percent). However, when only food commercials are compared, U.S. children's commercial are more likely to portray the uniqueness appeal than that of China (34.0 percent vs. 18.2 percent). Therefore, both H6a and H6b are supported when only comparing the commercials on food product from the two countries.

Economic development

Given that China is a relatively less developed country, it was hypothesized that a higher percent of Chinese children's commercials would include product benefit appeals (effectiveness, health, economy, or convenience). The data show that this was true in cases of health and convenience appeals. 38.6 percent of Chinese children's commercials emphasize the health appeal compared to 7.0 percent of U.S. commercials. 6.1 percent of Chinese children's commercials focus on convenience compared to 2.0 percent for ads from the U.S. Commercials in neither country emphasizes effectiveness. In addition, commercials in the two countries are equally likely to emphasize economy. Therefore H7 was partially supported.

Social factors

❏ *One-child policy*

Children's commercials in both China and the United States portray very little scholastic (1.5 percent vs. 1.6 percent) or athletic activities (2.3 percent vs. 2.0 percent). Therefore, neither H8a nor H8b was supported. That is, more scholastic or less athletic activities in Chinese commercials were not found.

❏ *Ethnic groups*

It was hypothesized that a lower percent of Chinese children's commercials would include ethnic groups than those of the United States. The data show that none of the Chinese children commercials include ethnic (non-Han races) models, although a few (6.1 percent) contain Western models. U.S. children's commercials, on the other hand, often utilize ethnic models, including Black (30.4 percent), Asian (7.0 percent), and Hispanic (5.4 percent). So H9 was supported by the current sample.

Discussion

Based on previous cross-national studies, it was hypothesized that commercials are a reflection of the cultural, social and economic contexts where the commercials are developed and broadcast. That is, major differences between China and the United States in cultural, economic, and social factors will lead to different content being portrayed in children's commercials. A look at the findings from this study reveals that this is generally the case. When using children's commercials from the United States as a benchmark, Chinese children's commercials, to a great extent, reflect China's traditional culture values and its social and economic conditions. This is especially true after controlling for the product category factor. Specifically, both presentation mode and information content of the ads reflect China's high uncertainty avoidance tendency. The lesser portrayal of fun/happiness and adventure and the higher usage of related settings, music, and animation are consistent with China's collectivism tradition. A greater usage of males as models, spokespersons, and voice-overs demonstrates that in media masculinity is still emphasized in today's China. Finally, a higher portrayal of the popularity appeal and a lesser portrayal of the uniqueness appeal in Chinese children's commercials reflect its face-saving (Confucius dynamism) tradition.

A surprising finding regarding the influence of culture on children's commercial content involves the power distance dimension. Counter to expectations, Chinese children's commercials are less likely to use an adult spokes person/character or adult voice-over than those in the United States. This is inconsistent with the fact that China has traditionally been a society with high power distance and older people are respected as authority figures. This unexpected finding is probably due to at least two factors. First, there may be an increasing awareness among advertisers that many young Chinese consumers are turned off by the bossy tone of many ads, a bad habit that is blamed on China's authoritarian political environment. Second, and seemingly more important, the one-child policy in China may be changing the traditional status of older people in China. That is, since each family can only have one child, Chinese people have become focused on the development of children and the serving of their needs. Given the fact that the next generation of each family is just one individual, the power and importance of children is heightened. Thus, one might conclude that TV advertising's less portrayal of adults and more of children is a reflection of power shifting in today's China.

Children's commercials in China are also a reflection of its economic development. As a less developed country, Chinese commercials are more likely to emphasize basic product benefits than those in the United States. The hypotheses about the impact of social factors on children's commercials received mixed results. There was not a significant difference in the portrayal of scholastic and athletic/exercise activities, but this may be due to the "floor effect" — these activities are portrayed little in both countries and therefore lack statistical power. The virtual omission of China's ethnic groups in its commercials, however, is consistent with China's government policy that emphasizes similarities rather than differences among all members of the population. As popular political propaganda says, "Everyone in China is a member of the big family." So unlike in the U.S. where advertisers regularly represent several ethnic groups in commercials, those in China tend to avoid this practice.

As a cultural artifact, Chinese children's commercials seem to represent a meeting place where traditional Chinese values and Western values intermingle, even seemingly clash. In this study, Chinese traditional values are still heavily portrayed in children's commercials in China, suggesting that the Chinese society as a whole and the Chinese advertising industry specifically are still trying to pass on to Chinese children its traditional values. These "cultural education efforts" through commercials probably take place unknowingly as members of the older generation in China routinely hand down their traditional values to children through various communications channels including television. The "cultural education effort" can also be practiced intentionally as the Advertising Law encourages positive education of the younger generation through television advertising. This will be discussed in detail in the coming chapter.

However, the findings also suggest that the Chinese culture seems to be changing as mirrored in these sample advertisements. For example, the minor usage of adults as spokespersons and voice-overs hints that the Chinese culture is adapting to its new social reality of one child per family. This greater elevation of the stature of the child vis-à-vis the adult is not unlike the family situation in the U.S. where the child is increasingly the focus of the household. Whether this change is due to any influence from the West in addition to the dramatic shift to one-child families in China is not discernable from the data. But as noted, there is a tendency among Chinese youth to favor Western lifestyles, and they may be learning them from mass media such as TV advertising and passing them on to their families in some form of reverse socialization, that is, teaching consumer behavior to the parents.

There is also more direct evidence in these findings of the entry of Western culture, and more importantly, it appears to conflict while coexist with traditional Chinese cultural values. As an example, the percentage of children's commercials that portray the popularity appeal, a traditional Chinese value, is consistently higher in China across both food and non-food products than that in the United States. But analyses also show that the uniqueness appeal, a typical Western value, is equally portrayed in the children's non-food commercials of both countries. (One might expect that a lower percent of Chinese children's commercials would demonstrate the uniqueness appeal.) These findings regarding uniqueness and popularity demonstrate a changing face of Chinese culture: China still holds on to traditional values such as universal acceptance or popularity, but also is beginning to assimilate Western values by emphasizing the unparalleled nature of a product or the uniqueness appeal among non-food products.

Appendix 8-1: Methodology of a content analysis study of children's commercials

One week every six months during an 18-month period (1998–1999) was chosen as a research time hoping to capture the true nature of television advertising in both countries. This simultaneous recording enabled the investigators to compare content difference in the commercials between the two countries while controlling for variance caused by time difference. Choosing six-month intervals was mainly based on observation in a pilot study that many Chinese commercials are aired as long as six months without any change (which is rarely the case in the U.S.). The time periods for sampling commercials in both countries included both weekday afternoons and weekend mornings. An examination of the Beijing TV Guide suggested that weekday afternoons and weekend mornings, like in the U. S., are the primary times when children's TV programs are broadcasted.

Five Chinese televisions channel — Channels One (CCTV-1) and Two (CCTV-2) of the China Central Television, Channels One (Beijing TV-1) and Two (Beijing TV-2) of Beijing Television, and Channel One of Beijing Cable Television (BCTV Cable1) — were selected for this analysis. Beijing was chosen as a research site to be fairly representative of the big cities in China. It is also the location of 14 out of the top 17 multinational ad agencies in China. The five selected channels cover around 80% of children's television programming in the Beijing area. In addition, Beijing local stations have the highest advertising revenue among all the local stations in China. Another important reason to choose Beijing as the research site is because Beijing-area television stations have the most stringent censorship policies. Generally, if a TV commercial has been approved by a Beijing station, stations elsewhere are not likely to reject it. Therefore, those commercials that are aired in Beijing are also very likely to be broadcast throughout the country. The four U.S. television-broadcasting systems selected were ABC, FOX, Nickelodeon and WB Kids, which broadcast nationally around 90% of children television programming in the United States during the research period.

All the commercials that aired right before, during, or right after children programming were videotaped and then analyzed. Two coders, an American male and a Chinese female, both fluent in Chinese and English and unaware of the purpose of the study, were hired to analyze the commercials. They were first trained to grasp the operationalizations of the variables in a pilot study. The variables included activity, animation, information content, models, music, settings, spokespersons/characters, style of display, values/appeals, and voice-overs. Except for ethnic status of models and expert-like spokespersons/characters, all other operationalizations were adapted from previous work. Based on the operationalizations, the two coders coded each commercial independently. In addition, the two coders also recorded the station where a commercial was broadcast, the length of the commercial, and the name of the product being advertised. In the cases where the coders disagreed, they examined the commercial together, discussed the disagreement, and made the final decision. Given the categorical nature of the data, cross-tab analysis was used to compare the frequency difference between U.S. and Chinese commercials and to test the proposed hypotheses.

Chapter 9

Regulating Children's Advertising in China

In the previous chapter, we examined the content of children's television commercials in China and found that they reflect both traditional Chinese values and Western values. In this chapter, we are going to review the rules and regulations governing advertising messages in China. We'll introduce the existing advertising ordinance and examine how it is interpreted. We'll also observe the censorship system of advertisements in China and discuss the advertising executions that have violated the *Advertising Law of the People's Republic of China*, enacted on February 1, 1995. In the last section of this chapter, we will discuss the self-regulation standards adopted by the advertising industry in China and compare them with the international code of practice.

Overview of existing advertising ordinance in China

Advertising is a carefully regulated industry in China (Cheng, 2000). China announced its *Advertising Law* on October 27, 1994 at the 10th session of the Standing Committee of the Eighth National People's Congress, and the *Advertising Law* went into effect on February 1, 1995 (Asia Law and Practice Limited, 1994). For a review of the evolution and major changes in advertising regulations and laws in China, see the works done by Hong Cheng and others (Cheng, 1996; Cheng, 1997b; Zhang, 2001). Between 1949, when the People's Republic was founded and 1966, when the Cultural Revolution (1966–1976) was started, there was not any national advertising regulation in China. All regulations concerning advertising were made by local governments. During the Cultural Revolution (1966–1976), all those regulations disappeared, together with virtually the entire advertising industry in the country (Cheng, 2000; Xu, 1990). On September 15, 1980, the Chinese State

Council formally announced that the State Administration of Industry and Commerce (SAIC) would be the official body in China to administer advertising. The decision reflected that the Chinese government's recognition of advertising as primarily a business activity (HKU Book, forthcoming). From 1979 when advertising came back to life in China to 1995 when the *Advertising Law* was enforced, the advertising industry in China was mainly guided by three major sets of regulations, and enriched by some additional detailed rules. In February 1982, the State Council promulgated the first set of national regulations for advertising, *the Interim Regulations for Advertising Management.* In December 1987, the *Interim Regulations for Advertising Management* was replaced by the *Regulations for Advertising Management.* Its interpretation was stipulated in the *Detailed Rules on the Implementation of the Regulations for Advertising Management* (Zhang, 2001). In 1993, the SAIC issued the *Interim Regulations on the Advertising Agency System* (Ha, 1996). The *Interim Regulations on the Advertising Agency System* became effective in July 1993 in Guangzhou, and in October 1993 in fifty other cities all over China (China Advertising, 1994). The objectives of this set of regulations are: (1) to clean up the messy advertising market environment, (2) to suppress unfair competition, (3) to protect consumer rights, and (4) to protect domestic products (Ha, 1996). In the *Interim Regulations on the Advertising Agency System*, the SAIC was authorized to issue disciplinary warnings and impose penalties in the case of any advertising violations (Articles 3, 14, and 27).

Concurrent with the promulgation of the *Interim Regulations on the Advertising Agency System* in 1993, the State Administration for Industry and Commerce promulgated the *Interim Advertising Censorship Standards.* The censorship standards were implemented first in six cities in southern Guangdong, and later in other provinces (Ha, 1996). The standards consist of sixteen articles and 125 sections, initially applicable to advertisements in the three major media namely, television, radio and newspapers. Later, the standards were extended to all media (State Administration for Industry and Commerce and State Planning Committee, 1993a).

Article 5 of the Censorship Standards stipulates the regulation of children's advertising. Children's advertising is defined as 'advertising of

products to be used by children or advertising using children as models'
(State Administration for Industry and Commerce and State Planning
Committee, 1993b). Accordingly, Children's advertisements would
violate the standards if they:

1. are harmful to children's mental and physical health or moral standards;
2. induce children to put pressure on parents to buy the advertised products;
3. reduce children's respect for their elders or friendly behavior;
4. interrupt parents' or elders' education of their children;
5. instill in children a sense of superiority or inferiority from owning or not owning an advertised product;
6. use child models to demonstrate a product in a capacity exceeding that of an average child of that age;
7. show acts that children should not be doing alone;
8. cause children to act or behave badly;
9. deceive children by using descriptions beyond the judgement capacity of children.
10. use the names, the identities or images of teachers, educators, writers of children's literature, or child celebrities to endorse products.

Vulgar and pornographic descriptions are strictly prohibited also
(Ha, 1996). In Western countries such as the United States, regulations
of children's advertising mainly aims at protecting children from
misleading advertising because of their presumed lack of competence to
understand advertising and make judgements about a product
(Lichtenberger, 1986). In China, the censorship standards focus more
on the cultural impact of advertising to children. The Chinese definition
of children's advertising is broader than that used in the Western societies
as it includes adult products that use children as models in advertisements
(Ha, 1996).

In October 1994, the Chinese government formulated the
Advertising Law effective February 1, 1995 (Asia Law and Practice
Limited, 1994). It is important to bear in mind that the *Advertising Law*
did not replace the 1987's *Regulations for Advertising Management* and
the 1993's *Interim Advertising Censorship Standards*. They are still in use

as "an essential supplement and operational guidelines to the *Advertising Law*" (Zhang, 2001, p. 14). This is confirmed in our interview with SAIC officials in Shanghai (Ban, 2002). With a total of 49 articles, the *Advertising Law* consists of six chapters: General Provisions, Contents of Advertisements, Advertising Activities, Advertisement Examination, Legal Responsibilities, and Supplementary Provisions. The advertising content is governed by the advertising standards stipulated in the Content of Advertisements chapter. The SAIC continued to maintain the advertising censorship system to prevent false advertising and illegal promotional activities.

The *Advertising Law* does not have separate articles specifically dealing with children's advertising. The protection of children is indirectly implied in Article 8 of Chapter 2, which states that advertisements may not be harmful to the physical and mental health of minors and the disabled. Article 8 basically requires that advertising to young audiences must conform to positive social standards.

Referring to Article 2 of the *Protecting the Minors Law*, the term 'minors' refers to any citizen under the age of 18. Article 3 of the *Protecting the Minors Law* stipulates that the nation, the society, the school, and the family are responsible for educating the minors on ideology, culture, discipline and legal matters. Minors should be taught about patriotism, collectivism, internationalism, and communism. Furthermore, minors should be taught to love the country, love the people, love to work, love science, and love socialistic values. Also, they should be protected from capitalism, feudalism, and other corruptive ideology. Article 10 of the *Protecting the Minors Law* requires that parents and other guardians adopt appropriate methods to teach young people healthy thoughts and good behaviors. They should encourage young people to participate in activities that are beneficial to their mental and physical health. They should prevent and prohibit young people from smoking, drinking, gambling, wandering, taking illegal drugs, and being prostitutes. Article 26 of the *Protecting the Minors Law* stipulates that food, toys, tools and entertainment facilities for children must not be harmful to children's safety and health. One implication of this article is that advertisements for children's products should present the functions, quality, usage and other related information in a clear and understandable manner for children. Sensitive products including tobacco and alcohol should not use children models in their advertisements (Zhang, 2001).

The current *Advertising Law* does not have specific rules about regulating Internet advertising that targets at children. Some countries have developed guidelines for Internet advertising on children's web sites and online services target at children, for example in the U.S. (Children's Advertising Review Unit, 2003). There is certainly room for improvement in China's regulation of children's advertising in the new media age.

Advertising targeting at children, like other advertisements, also needs to follow the regulations governing the content of advertisements stipulated in the *Advertising Law*. In accordance with the Law, an advertisement shall not involve any of the following circumstances:

- Using the national flag, emblem or anthem;
- Using the names of State authorities;
- Using words such as 'the Sate-level', 'the highest-grade', or 'the best';
- Hindering social stability or endangering the safety of the person or property, or harming the public interests;
- Hindering the public order or violating the sound social morals;
- Containing information suggesting pornography, superstition, terror, violence or hideousness;
- Containing information of ethnic, racial, religious or sexual discrimination;
- Hindering the protection of the environment or natural resources; or
- Containing deceptive data or statistical information;
- Belittling the products of other manufacturers and dealers or services of other providers;
- (in an advertisement for pharmaceuticals or medical apparatus) the use of the name or image of a medical research institution, academic organization, medical institution or of an expert, a doctor or patient as proof.

Examples of controversial television commercials targeting at children

The advertising industry in China criticized the *Advertising Law* for its vagueness that would create an atmosphere of confusion among advertisers and agencies concerning the operational definitions of the new law, and which types of advertisements would be accepted and which rejected (Chadwick, 1997). For clarification we will present some examples to illustrate what types of content are considered inappropriate or appropriate for children's advertisements in China. Their sources are books about advertising regulations in China and personal interviews with advertising agency personnel in Shanghai.

The following examples of television commercials are cited from the book *Advertising Law and Cases for Discussion* (Zhu, 2000). We are not certain whether these commercials have actually been broadcast in the media. They may represent commercials that failed to pass the *Advertising Law* and hence never been shown on TV. Or they may represent commercials that have been broadcast and later being pulled out because of their problematic content.

Example 1: In a pharmaceutical commercial, the narration goes, "The child is sick; give him a shot ..." The child refuses, "Oh, no, no." "Give him medicine ..." The child refuses again, "Oh, no, no." "He doesn't like the pain or the taste." The commercial then shows the frustrated mother kneeling on the floor, begging the child, "Oh, my dear, what do you want?" An imported medicine appears and it solves the problem.

This commercial is considered a violation of Article 8 as it features the child as a spoiled emperor, demanding submission from the parents. It also portrays the parents in a passive and inadequate role.

Example 2: A soft drink claims that it can boost the intelligence of children. The commercial shows a little boy lying in his mother's arms. He says, "My grandpa is a manager, and my dad is a manager. When I grow up, I would like to be a manager, too."

This commercial also is considered a violation of Article 8 because it misleads children into believing that using the product will enhance their intelligence and their future career. Although it is not mentioned in the book, we think that this commercial is also ideologically incorrect. Glorifying the managerial class in the society carries undesirable capitalistic overtones.

Example 3: A commercial features a group of students going home from school. All of them are enjoying soft drinks, except a boy dressed in shabby clothes. The group is singing and playing with high spirit, leaving the boy behind. The commercial ends with a close-up of the boy, looking depressed and disappointed.

This commercial is considered violating Article 8 because it stresses the visual differences between the "haves" and the "have-nots." It implies that a child without the product will be isolated from his or her peers. So, the commercial also violated Article 5 of the *Interim Advertising Censorship Standards* by instilling a sense of inferiority from not owning the advertised product.

In the same book, it also suggests that the following advertising content will violate Article 8 of the *Advertising Law*:

- showing children fighting to get access to favorite food or toys
- showing children keeping products to themselves and refusing to share
- showing children not paying respect to others
- showing children becoming energetic after taking certain pills, even without eating or sleeping
- guaranteeing that children get outstanding examination results
- showing children smoking, drinking, wandering on the streets, gambling, or performing violent acts

The book also cited a few examples of "good" and "culturally appropriate" children's advertisements.

Example 1: In an almond drink commercial, a girl prepares the drink and serves it to her grandfather. This commercial is good because the girl shows respect and caring for the elderly in her family.

Example 2: In a series of commercials for an electrical appliance company, the cartoon characters (twin brothers) risk their lives to save a child who accidentally fell into the river, pack the wound of a bird with great care, and stand up to criticize merchants selling low-quality fake products. These commercials are considered good because the characters demonstrate bravery, kindness, justice, and purity.

Example 3: In an ice-cream commercial, the slogan goes that "You should eat it only once a day." The commercial is considered appropriate because it does not over-promote the product irrationally and helps children to develop a good eating habit.

In the book, it also notes that many public service announcements are good for children because they teach them socially responsible behaviors such as protecting the environment and care for the community.

The following example was given by J. Walter Thompson, an international advertising agency, in 1997 (Weber, 1999). The advertising agency produced a commercial for De Beers, a multinational diamond distributor. The commercial starts with a scenario of two young children. A young boy places a ring made of grass on the finger of a young girl. The commercial then cuts to a scene where both of them have grown up. The young man is placing a diamond ring on the young lady's finger on their wedding day. The commercial was initially rejected because it featured "puppy love." The scenario was considered inappropriate because children should focus their lives on education and family. The agency later changed the opening of the commercial to include a wide shot of a group of young children playing under a tree and it was successful in reducing the censors' concerns. In this example, we notice that even though the commercial is targeting adults, it needs to follow the *Advertising Law* regarding children as children images are shown. The minimal changes to the advertisement and subsequent approval show the ambiguity of the interpretation of advertising content by Chinese censors (Weber, 1999).

The following examples were given to us by a multinational advertising agency in Shanghai. The first three commercials did not obtain approval for their storyboards and therefore did not appear on TV. The last commercial was initially rejected but later aired after approval.

Example 1: A children's food commercial featuring Santa Claus for Christmas greeting was not approved in 2001. This was because Christmas was not an official holiday in China and Santa was not considered as an appropriate celebrity figure for children due to its religious origin.

Example 2: A children's drink commercial featuring dinosaurs conquering a dream city in a surreal setting did not get the approval because of its scary scenes and the anti-social behavior of destroying the city.

Example 3: An animated commercial featuring a teenager's neck stretching out for food and becoming very long. The commercial failed to obtain approval because of its unreal scene.

Example 4: A milk powder commercial featured a boy climbing up a ladder to a spaceship and reaching out for the stars. The storyboard was initially not approved. After a series of negotiation, it finally obtained the green light to be shown on TV.

In order to understand the interpretation of good behaviors in children's commercials, we discussed a McDonald's commercial launched in China in 2002 during our interview with a SAIC officer responsible for advertising censorship in Shanghai (Ban, 2002). The commercial featured a boy about four-years-old playing peek-a-boo with his dad. The boy seized every chance to reach out for a French fry when his dad covered the face. The boy seemed to enjoy the game a lot but the last shot hinted that it was the food that kept the game alive. We asked whether the boy was behaving badly. The answer was a definite "no" because the family scene was considered light-hearted and positive in manner. We also discussed a McDonald's commercial launched in Hong Kong that the client decided to pull out after showing it for a week (Chan, 1997). The commercial featured a boy about nine years old. He told mum that dad promised to bring him to McDonald's, and then pulled the same trick on dad. The parents finally discovered the truth when they were at the restaurant. The SAIC officer we interviewed in Shanghai said that this commercial would not pass through the censorship because it demonstrated the immoral behavior of telling lies. The accounting director of the advertising agency in Shanghai agreed with his point of view.

Censorship of advertisements

According to the *Advertising Law*, the content of advertisements is to be censored prior to dissemination in the media by relevant administrative authorities-in-charge. When an advertiser applies for approval of an advertisement, he shall submit relevant supporting documents to the advertising censorship authorities. These authorities shall make a censorship decision in accordance with relevant laws. Figure 9-1 shows the organization structure of the censorship authorities. Censorship authorities are responsible for approval of business establishments engaging in the advertising industry, setting of advertising standards, giving instructions on censorship, providing guidance for the advertising industry, initiating and verifying advertisements with illegal claims (China Advertising Yearbook, 2001). As advertisements are censored at the local levels, advertising agency people have been complaining about the confusion arising as different regions interpret the *Advertising Law* differently (Miao, 1995). To overcome the regional differences in censorship standards, advertisers would decide to launch advertising campaigns in major provinces such as Beijing, Guangzhou, or Shanghai

Figure 9-1: Organization structure of the censorship authorities

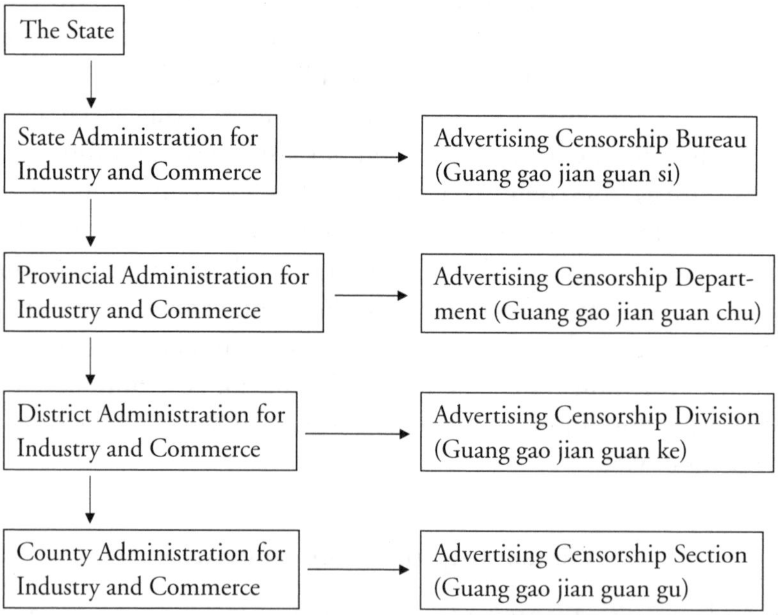

Source: China Advertising Yearbook (2001).

where the implementation of regulations is more consistent (Xu, 1992). The SAIC attempts to standardize the censoring process, but the cultural diversity within the nation has made it a difficult task (Xinhua News Agency, 2000).

However, according to our interviews with SAIC officials and advertising agency personnel, we have noticed that the actual censorship practice is quite complicated. In addition to the SAIC office for advertising censorship, there are at least three more other groups of gatekeepers housed in various organizations. The following paragraphs will discuss who they are and what their roles are in the advertising censorship system.

1. Advertising examiners: According to the current regulations, each business establishment engaged in advertising should employ at least two advertising examiners and two senior advertising examiners. These people need to pass an examination set up by the SAIC and obtain a license (Figure 9-2). They also need to attend regular briefing and training

Figure 9-2: The license of an Advertising Examiner

sessions about the new development of the advertising regulations
organized by SAIC. Their roles are to act as internal auditors that help
the business establishments to enhance the understanding of specific
requirements and interpretation of the *Advertising Law*. They are
supposed to vet the advertising content to make sure it abides with the
law. However, our interview with the advertising agency indicated that
these people played minor roles in the censorship process and existed in
name only.

2. Advertising consultants: The China Advertising Association
established an information consultant center that provides legal
consultancy services for advertising agencies. Upon the commission of
the advertising agencies, they will examine the advertising content of
the television commercials (in the form of storyboards, rough cuts or
final reels), radio commercials, print and outdoor advertisements. The
China Advertising Association has both national office and regional
offices. For national campaigns, advertising agencies usually send the
advertisements to the national office in Beijing. For regional campaigns,
the advertisements will be sent to the respective local offices for pre-
screening advice. On examination of the advertising content, the China
Advertising Association will issue a certificate of advertising consultancy.
If the Association sees no problem with the advertisement, the certificate
will state that the advertisement does not violate the *Advertising Law*
and related regulations and can be released in the media. The approval
by the China Advertising Association is considered to be equivalent to
that of the SAIC for some major media.

3. Media gatekeepers: Ultimately, an advertisement needs to appear
in a certain medium. People in the media sometimes act as the final
gatekeepers in the censorship process. According to our interview with
advertising agency people in China, the media sometimes reject an
advertisement even if it has obtained a certificate of approval from the
national office of the China Advertising Association.

The whole censorship process is bureaucratic and extremely time
consuming and costly. Each approval decision will normally take a week.
If an advertisement is not approved, it usually comes with a stated reason.
The advertising agency people will discuss the decision with the client.
They can propose some amendments and resubmit it for approval or

they can negotiate for a change in the decision by providing further substantiation. For example, the milk powder commercial featuring a boy climbing up a ladder was first rejected by the media because the act was considered as dangerous. The advertising agency argued it differently. Finally, the commercial was allowed to air for a probation period of three months.

The advertising agency people have been strongly critical of the subjective judgement involved in the censorship process because it has caused much stress. The system may also invite unfair competition as some people can maneuver through 'guanxi' or even bribery in order to gain approval or obtain approval before the normal deadline.

From our interview with the SAIC official in Shanghai, we learned that the censorship system is not fully implemented in all media. Occasionally the media accept advertisements without any approval documents. That's why the SAIC has set up an advertising-monitoring unit to constantly sample-check advertisements appearing in different media. For example, the Shanghai SAIC set up thresholds for the violation rate for different media. The thresholds for first-tier media (major TV stations and newspapers), second-tier media (e.g. newspaper with smaller circulation), and third-tier media (e.g. specialized magazines) are 2 percent, 4 percent and 6 percent respectively of the total number of advertisements shown in that medium. When a certain medium attains a violating rate above the threshold level in a sampling period say one week, the SAIC will begin to monitor that medium closely or give it verbal warning.

Illegal advertisements in China

In 2000, the censorship authorities found 66,824 cases that violating the *Advertising Law*, compared to 51,494 cases found in 1999. Approximately 100 million yuan in fines were imposed. Altogether 693 business establishments were compelled to discontinue their businesses temporarily, and another 262 business establishments had their business registration licenses revoked (China Advertising Yearbook, 2001). According to Article 37 of the *Advertising Law*, the SAIC is authorized to charge advertisers, advertising agencies, or media owners fines of up to five times the cost of their advertising spending if an advertisement is found illegal. In addition, the advertisers have to put in the same amount of advertising fee to run corrective advertising for false claims. For the more serious breaches, there is also scope for criminal prosecution (Sdinfo Net, 2002).

Table 9-1 summarizes the profile of the illegal cases found in 2000. Illegal advertisements involved mainly pharmaceuticals, medical services, and food. These three product categories accounted for over one third of illegal cases. In view of the prevalence of problematic medical ads, some provinces have decided to ban all ads about medicine and medical institutes. For example, the SAIC of Hunan Province banned medical institutes ads in all media from February 11 to April 10, 2002 (China Media Net, 2002a). The SAIC of Shanghai banned all medical services ads and medicine ads in all media for three months from April 18, 2002. It found that 362 out of 453 advertisements monitored on television, radio and in newspapers fell short of the legal requirement of being "true, healthy, scientific and accurate." (*Jiefang Daily*, 2002). Nevertheless, the situation did not improve. According to a report of the SAIC of Guangzhou, 98 percent of the medical services ads in the city in a routine censorship exercise violated the advertising regulations (*Xin kuai News*, 2002). Similarly, the SAIC of Beijing found nearly 100 percent of medical services ads in a routine check violating the regulations (China Media Net, 2002b).

Some of the illegal advertisements for medicines and medical institutes are found in media targeting children and the youth. Most of them are medicines and medical services advertisements claiming to enhance growth, enhance memory or take care of various health problems of students such as shortsightedness. For example, an advertisement in a youth magazine claimed that two sisters took the medicine and grew taller by 18 and 23 cm. A print advertisement in a computer magazine claimed that a pill, developed by American genetic experts, enhanced growth by 6 to 14 cm. A print advertisement in a children's magazine claimed that a multi-function eye massage machine improves eyesight and memory. These advertisements took advantage of the eagerness of the parents and children to excel in physical and cognitive development.

Advertisements appearing in outdoor media and in printed materials

Table 9-1: Profile of illegal advertisements investigated in 2000

Illegal ads	No. of case	%
By product category		
Medicine	13,986	20.9
Medical services	5,983	9.0
Food	5,213	7.8
Electrical appliance	2,104	3.2
Cosmetics	1,518	2.3
Wines	1,424	2.1
Real estate	1,150	1.7
Medical equipment	1,149	1.7
Insecticides	507	0.8
Cigarettes	469	0.7
Finance	236	0.4
Others	33,085	49.5
By media		
Outdoor	25,719	38.5
Print	19,619	29.4
Newspaper	4,673	7.0
Television	2,499	3.7
Radio	810	1.2
Magazines	483	0.7
Others	13,021	19.5
By nature		
Fake ads	11,199	16.8
Others	55,625	83.2
By illegal party		
Advertisers	36,470	54.6
Publishers	11,034	16.5
Marketers	8,512	12.7
Others	10,808	16.2
By geographical regions		
Shandong	8,377	12.5
Zhejiang	6,060	9.1
Liaoning	4,742	7.1
Shichuan	4,492	6.7
Jiangsu	4,062	6.1
Guangdong	3,613	5.4
Henan	3,308	5.0
Others	32,170	48.2
Number of illegal ads examined by SAIC	66,824	100.0

Source: China Advertising Yearbook (2001).

other than newspapers and magazines accounted for two-third of illegal cases. Advertisements in major mass media (TV, radio and newspapers) contributed to about one-tenth of illegal cases, indicating that these media are well regulated. About one-sixth of illegal cases involved false claims in the advertising content while the rest of the cases involved illegal advertising practices. In view of the large amount of illegal outdoor advertising that usually is placed by the clients directly (rather than by ad agencies), the percentage of illegal cases involving advertising agencies are low. Illegal advertising prevails in provinces where advertising is less developed, with the exception of Guangdong Province. This situation confirms our previous discussion that cities where advertising is highly developed such as Beijing and Shanghai usually have a stricter control of advertising standards.

Cheng (2003) conducted a content analysis of 43 illegal advertising cases that occurred between 1995 and 1997, and found that the illegal advertising cases were initially challenged by three sources: consumers, competitors, and/or SAIC staff. Compared to SAIC staff (65%) and consumers (30%), competitors' initiations (5%) were rare. SAIC staff played a dominant role in the verification process to determine whether the advertising claims were true or not. About three-quarters of all verifications for illegal advertising cases were conducted by SAIC staff. Consumers verified a small portion of the advertisements (12%). The court (7%), experts (4%), and the police (2%) were even less frequently involved in the verification of advertising claims.

The same study also identified eight common techniques employed in illegal advertisements. Among these eight techniques, providing false information (41%) and using puffery (25%) were the most common. Other less frequently employed techniques included understating certain information (8%), the unawareness of political inappropriateness (6%), insensitivity of cultural inappropriateness (6%), illegal sponsorship (6%), belittling competitors (4%), and providing counterfeiting documentation to pass censorship (4%) (Cheng, 2003).

The frequent involvement of SAIC staff in the initiation and verification phases of handling illegal advertising cases demonstrates the vital role the SAIC plays in the implementation of the *Advertising Law* in China (Cheng, 2003). Many potentially illegal advertisements were first discovered by SAIC staff members in their routine checks of the advertising content of media or the performances of advertising agencies. Compared to many western societies, the notion of "consumer rights" is not popular in China. The China Consumers Association, the nation's only consumer protection agency, conducted a survey of 4,000 consumers in Beijing in 1994 and found that when rights were violated, 40 percent of the consumers would backtrack and accept defeat. Only 13 percent would complain to the consumer associations (Chinese Consumer Newspaper, 1994). In a survey of 500 consumers in Beijing in 1996 (Chan, 1998) twenty-one percent said they would complain to the consumer associations at various levels if they were not satisfied with their purchases. A majority of them said they would bad-mouth the products and advise friends not to purchase them. Only eight percent would complain to organizations responsible for regulating advertising (Chan, 1998). However, we expect that Chinese consumers will play an increasingly important role in the initiation of challenges to advertisements. For example, a father of a two-year-old boy sued South Korean manufacturer LG in May 1999. He charged that an air-conditioner TV commercial featuring a fire-breathing monster was too frightening and sought 30,000 yuan in damages (Wiseman, 1999). The China Consumer Association has set up events such as "Month for Disclosing Deceptive Ads" (*jie huang yue*) to encourage consumers to report deceptive ads (China Business, 2001). Usually, consumers that have been deceived by the advertisements report the experience. Instead of filing suits in the court, they tend to voice their complaints to the SAIC. The very low involvement of competitors in the initiation phase of challenging illegal advertising cases is probably due to the restrictions, if not prohibition, of comparative advertising in the *Advertising Law* (Article 21) (Cheng, 2003).

Self-regulation of children's advertising

Self-regulation in the advertising sector is the recognition by the advertising industry (advertisers, agencies and the media) that advertising should comply to a set of ethical rules; namely, that it should be legal, decent, honest and truthful, prepared with a sense of social responsibility to the consumer and to society as a whole, and with due respect to the rules of fair competition. This is achieved through the establishment of a set of rules and principles of best practice to which members of the advertising industry voluntarily agree to be bound.

In China, the China Advertising Association is the official association representing the advertising industry. The Association was established in December 1983. The members are mainly large advertising agencies, advertising departments of the major media, universities with advertising educational programs, and large and medium-sized corporations with advertising departments. It developed the *Self-regulatory Guidelines for Spiritual Civilization in Advertising* in 1997 (China Advertising Association, 2002). The main objective of the Guidelines is to raise the spiritual civilization standards in advertisements. "Spiritual civilization," a more-than-a-decade-long political jargon in China, refers to, among other things, the love for the motherland, loyalty to the Party, care for fellow citizens, diligence and honesty at work, and concern for the environment (Poole, 1996). Thus, according to the Guidelines, "Spiritual civilization" refers to moral standards in a socialist context. All members of the China Advertising Association are required to follow the Guidelines. Specifically, the Guidelines require that all advertisements should:

- encourage healthy consumption and discourage conspicuous consumption
- instill Chinese cultural values and enhance national pride and esteem
- promote scientific knowledge and discourage superstition
- be beneficial to the national construction and economic progress, and
- be beneficial to national sovereignty and unity.

Of importance to the subject of this book, Article 8 of the Guidelines stipulates that advertising should be beneficial to the physical and mental health of children. Advertisements for children's products and/or advertisements involving children models need to portray the children with good moral standards. The appearance of children and parents in such advertisements should demonstrate good manners and behaviors. The following content is prohibited:

- inducing children to put pressure on parents
- portraying children demonstrating disrespectful, unfriendly, or uncivilized manners and behaviors to their elders or other people
- instilling in children a sense of superiority or inferiority for owning a specific product
- deceiving children by using descriptions beyond their judgement capacity
- showing acts that children should not undertake alone
- portraying children smoking or drinking

Members who violate the Guidelines are subjected to penalties, including open criticism or even membership termination.

Table 9-2: Comparison of the Chinese Self-regulation Guidelines and the ICC Code of Advertising Practice regarding children's advertising

	Guidelines	ICC Code of Advertising Practice
Advertisements should not exploit the inexperience or credulity of minors	✔	✔
Price indication should not be misleading		✔
Advertisement should not understate the degree of skill or age level required to use or enjoy the product		✔
Advertisements should not have the effect of harming minors mentally, morally or physically	✔	✔
Advertisements should not suggest that possession or use of a product will give the child advantages over others, or that non-possession would have the opposite effect	✔	✔
Advertisements should not undermine the authority, responsibility, judgement or tastes of parents		✔
Advertisements should not include direct appeal to minors to persuade their parents or other adults to buy advertised products for them	✔	✔

In order to provide a better understanding of how China's self-regulation differs from other countries, we attempted to compare the Chinese Guidelines regarding advertising to children with parallel guidelines in the *International Code of Advertising Practice* (1997 edition) developed by the International Chamber of Commerce, which is an updated version of the original code first established in 1937 (International Chamber of Commerce, 2002). The Code has inspired many of the national self-regulatory codes currently in use in many countries, including the U.S., the UK and other European countries. The comparison is summarized in Table 9-2. Such a comparison indicates that China's Self-regulation Guidelines basically are in line with the ICC Code, with the exception of three items: the restriction on presentation of price information, the skill level for using the products, and the responsibility of parents.

Some conclusions

As advertising has developed rapidly in China in just the last two decades, advertising regulations are still in the process of evolution. Since the introduction of the *Advertising Law*, the advertising industry has been complaining about its vagueness and its openness to subjective interpretation. Obviously, the SAIC is the major party that performs the gatekeeper's role. There are also gatekeepers in advertising agencies and in the media. As the *Advertising Law* does not have a separate section that deals with children's advertising, it certainly has room for improvement. The gate-keeping function aims at maintaining truth and good moral behaviors in children's advertisements. The advertising industry is exercising self-regulation regarding children's advertisement. We have a feeling that the multinational advertising agencies are following the self-regulations closely while small-scale advertising agencies and local advertisers are not doing so. This can be seen from the large amount of illegal advertisements found by the censorship authorities. This pattern may also help to explain why many parents and children hold negative attitudes toward advertising. It's clear from the previous chapters that advertising exerts enormous impact on Chinese children, who are immature audience lacking the essential ability to judge the advertising content. Therefore, a well-defined advertising law is essential for the healthy growth of the advertising industry in China that focuses on children.

Chapter 10

Advertising to Children in China: Summary, Conclusions, and Implications

As this new millennium gets underway China is in the midst of an economic revolution in which it is changing from a State controlled economy to a market controlled economy. It is the new age of "McDonaldization" in which the Western world's brands have become the symbols of what's good, what's wanted, what's bought by Chinese consumers whose income is growing at an average annual rate far above consumers of any large nation. Using Beijing as an example, one Professor of Chinese Society and Professor of Anthropology at Harvard University describes the new China this way:

"Looming over Beijing's choking, bumper-to-bumper traffic, every tenth building seems to sport a giant neon sign advertising American wares: Xerox, Mobil, Kinko's, Northwest Airlines, IBM, Jeep, Gerber, even the Jolly Green Giant. American food chains and beverage are everywhere in central Beijing: Coca-Cola, Starbucks, Kentucky Fried Chicken, Haagen-Dazs, Dunkin' Donuts, Baskin-Robbins, Pepsi, TCBY, Pizza Hut, and of course McDonald's." (Watson, 2000, p. 120)

In effect, socialism is giving way to capitalism in China (although this certainly would not be the official Party line). Making money and spending money are in vogue, and nowhere more than within the typical urban family where one child — mandated by law — is in charge of the household's purse strings. In this new "filiarchy," which has virtually supplanted the traditional patriarchic family of China, Mom and Dad usually both work while their one child is busily spending or being the focus of spending around two-thirds of the household income (McNeal, 1999). Consequently, China's children, who constitute nearly a quarter of the world's population of children, are the center of attention for a wide range of domestic and global marketers who target them with a growing number of advertising messages.

The previous chapters of this book have given consideration to this new phenomenon — advertising to children in China — by presenting new research that was conducted in the environment of new China that describes this advertising and the responses to it by children and their parents. In this final chapter we want to pull together the essentials of the research findings, draw some conclusions from them, and make some suggestions about what they mean to the advertising community.

Summary

❑ *Chinese children's media and advertising experience*

First, in order for Chinese children to express opinions about advertising, they must have some experience with it and with the media in which it appears. They do. Most of them read magazines and newspapers five to six hours a week, listen to radio at least as much, and watch television around 17 hours a week on average. So, they are media savvy. As for advertising, there is some that targets them in print media, and more on radio, but the bulk of advertising that the children experience is on TV. On a typical day on Beijing's national TV the kids may experience 85 commercials during the after school broadcasts to kids from 5:30 to 7 o'clock. That amounts to almost one ad per minute. If they watch 17 hours per week, which is the average according to our measures, they may see one thousand ads per week or 50,000 per year!

Chances are that only one-third of the TV commercials that Chinese children see are specifically for kids' products while two-thirds are for adult's products. This means that the children probably see ads for harmful products such as alcoholic beverages, personal care products such as cosmetics, toiletries and medicines, and for many durable goods such as cars, furniture, and appliances. Consequently, the children may gain knowledge of such items rather early in life, and perhaps contrary to the wishes of their parents. For example, probably many of the ads for medicines are illegal because they are false and misleading. Of the TV commercials that the children experience that are for products specifically targeted to them, the vast majority is for foods and beverages. And, again, some of these ads may be in spite of the wishes of many parents who worry about their children's diets. In sum, urban Chinese children have substantial experience with advertising and the media in which it appears.

❏ *Chinese children's perceptions of television advertising*

We have drawn together two tables to summarize the significant research findings presented in the previous chapters. Table 10-1 presents a summary analysis of Chinese children's perceptions of television advertising by three age groups — ages 6–7, 8–11, and 12–14. These age groups, suggested by John (1999), are based on the cognitive development levels of children as described in many previous research efforts. Also, age is the demographic variable most used by advertisers to segment children as media audiences. What is being suggested by these age groupings is as follows.

Children, ages 6–7, who are in the *perceptual stage* mainly make judgements of environmental objects based on their observable features (sensory responses) such as how an object feels, looks, sounds, tastes, and smells — not on any abstract reasoning. Thus, if a restaurant smells good to a child in this age group, it probably will receive a good evaluation, and if one bottle of soda that a child in this stage likes is taller (bigger) than another, the taller one is probably preferred. They may judge a brand of a product as good based on the colors in which it is printed, its advertised jingles, or simply how good the product tastes. Thus, they have superficial knowledge of marketplace objects such as products, advertisements, and stores, and make superficial judgements of these objects. Of course, such judgements do not mean they are wrong, but that they are likely different and less sophisticated than those of older children in the other two stages.

Children in this perceptual stage have little understanding of what TV commercials are, at most seeing some of them as funny messages that accompany the programs they watch. However, many are becoming aware of the purposes of advertising. Two third of them understood that television advertising wants them to buy things or tell their parents about the products. Some children in the perceptual stage think that they are supposed to check the advertised products at stores. Thus, it appears they see advertising as more of an adult thing, perhaps due in part to the majority of advertisements that accompany children's programs being for adult products and contain adult models. When given reasons for why they think TV stations broadcast commercials, they do say that making money is the main reason. This answer, however, may be chosen in great part due to the talk in new China about making money. To the extent they understand the concept of trust, they say they trust advertising, but the reality is they rely mainly on parents and teachers to help them know which ads are truthful. As objects, they both like and dislike TV ads, probably liking those few they pay attention to — those intended for children that are animated, funny, and provide information useful to children. They also say they like advertised as well as unadvertised products. Perhaps they are unable to classify products in this manner, and the mention of products brings to mind those products that satisfy their predominant needs.

Children, ages 8–11, are in the *analytical stage* and would be called brighter than those in the perceptual stage because they know more. For example, a 9-year-old is 50% more experienced than a 6-year-old, has a much greater memory storage based on the 50% additional experience, and has reasoning ability that often looks and sounds very much like an adult. It seems that there is a time, what some call the "one-hundred-month line," that divides child from adult, abstract thinker from concrete thinker, self-oriented person from other-oriented person. In the case of marketplace objects, this child can choose favorite brands, favorite stores, favorite advertisements, basing these judgements on a mind full of matter — knowledge and experience — rather than just how they sound, look or taste.

Regarding TV advertising, children in the analytical stage have a better understanding of it than the young ones, knowing that it introduces products, that it is product based, and that children are supposed to see the advertised products at stores and tell their parents about them. They pay more attention to ads than younger children, and make more judgements about their truthfulness, believing some are true, some are not. They rely on their own knowledge and experience, more than that of adults around them, to make these judgements. They know that stations carry the ads to make money, they like some, dislike some, and are neutral about some. Thus, they possess evaluative criteria for deciding about ads. Those they like are those that are informative, including PSA's, and they particularly like funny, animated commercials like the young kids, both groups having a strong need for play. They are generally neutral toward those ads with celebrity presenters. They think that advertised brands are better than unadvertised, perhaps due to their ability to discern ads intended for them as compared to the majority that is intended for adults.

Children in the *reflective stage*, those in the age group of 12–14, are even more advanced thinkers, advanced beyond the 100-month-line with another 50% or so of experience including experience with abstract thinking. Thus, a child in the perceptual stage might prefer an orange drink because it is in a big, colorful bottle. The child in the analytical stage might like it for these reasons, also, but additionally because it is reasonably priced. And the child in the reflective stage might like it for all these reasons but also because it is healthy and liked by mom. Thus, it might actually be difficult to classify any one child into one of these stages, but at least their degree of complex thinking and their taking the perspective of others, such as that of mom, can be used with some confidence.

These reflective children are able to reason that TV commercials are messages that promote products for them to buy. Thus, they are able to see the perspective of the marketer much more than children in the two younger groups, and reason that advertisers and TV broadcasters intend to make money. They watch TV ads sometimes, probably mainly those that target them, they believe some, don't believe others, and rely on the brand's reputation to decide if an ad is true or not. They neither like nor dislike commercials in general, and do like specific commercials that increase their knowledge, including PSAs, and are neutral toward commercials with celebrities. They are not for sure whether advertised or unadvertised brands are better since they recognize that ads are to sell products.

❏ *Chinese parents' attitudes toward television advertising*

Table 10-2 consists of a summary description of parents' views of advertising that is directed to their children as well as advertising in general. The parents described in this table are the parents of the children represented in Table 10-1. That is, the research efforts matched parents and children so that attitudes and behavior of children could be compared with those of their parents, and vice versa, in order to achieve a higher explanatory level. Thus, when it is stated, for example, that parents "seldom discuss commercials with children," it is the parents of the children in Table 10-1 to whom it refers.

Those parents with young children — with one child most likely — in the perceptual stage practice a high level of socio-oriented and a medium level of concept-oriented communications about consumption. This means that parents control the discussions between them and their children, seek obedience from the children, but seek some opinions from the child mainly about products for him or her. They seldom watch TV with their children or discuss TV commercials with them. They feel negative about TV advertising and particularly about ads that target their children. So, they exert a high level of control over the children's TV viewing and feel they influence how their children feel about the advertising on TV.

Parents of children in the analytical stage look very much like those with children in the perceptual stage. They are probably a bit less strict in communications with their children, watch TV with them a bit more, and are not so negative about TV advertising to the kids. In general, the parents seem to be granting somewhat more independence in thinking and action to those children ages 8–11.

For parents of those children in the age bracket, 12–14, the reflective stage, there's a lot more give and take between them and their children about consumption matters. Also, there is more co-viewing of TV between parents and children, but there seems to still be very little discussion of the commercials on TV. However, parents of reflective stage children show less negativism toward the commercials while still maintaining a high level of control on their kids' TV viewing, and feeling they influence their kids' attitudes toward TV advertising.

Table 10-1: Summary of Chinese children's perception of television advertising and brands by consumer socialization stage

Topic	Perceptual stage, 6–7 years	Analytical stage, 8–11 years	Reflective stage, 12–14 years
Understanding of what TV commercials are	Low, consider commercials as funny messages	Medium, consider commercials as messages that introducing products	Medium, more likely to consider commercials as messages that promote products
Understanding the purpose of TV commercials	High, believe commercials want them to buy the products or to tell parents about the products	Medium, some believe commercials want them to check the products at stores or to tell parents about the products	High, more likely believe commercials want them to buy the products than to tell parents about the products
Understanding why TV stations broadcast commercials	High, know TV stations broadcast commercials to make money or to sponsor the programs	High, know TV stations broadcast commercials to make money or to sponsor the programs	High, know TV stations broadcast commercials to make money or to sponsor the programs
Attention to TV commercials	Low, switch to other channels	Watch sometimes	Watch sometimes
Trust in TV commercials	Believe commercials are truthful	Believe some commercials are true and some are not	Believe some commercials are true and some are not
How to know which commercials are true and which are not	Rely on authority (parents, teachers)	Rely on user experience and brand equity	Rely mainly on brand equity
Attitude toward TV commercials	Strong bipolar attitude, some like very much and some dislike very much	Roughly equal proportion of those who like, dislike, or holding neutral attitude	neutral attitude, neither like nor dislike
Attitude toward commercials using different creative executions	Like commercials that increase the knowledge	Like commercials that increase the knowledge Like animated commercials, funny commercials and PSAs Neutral attitude toward commercials with celebrities	Like commercials that increase the knowledge Like PSAs Neutral attitude toward commercials with celebrities
Perception of advertised and non-advertised brands	Both are good	Advertised brands are better	Don't know which one is better

Table 10-2: Summary of Chinese parents' mediation of television viewing and perception of advertising by their children's consumer socialization stages

Topic	Parents with children at perceptual stage, 6–7 years	Parents with children at analytical stage, 8–11 years	Parents with children at reflective stage, 12–14 years
Parent-child communication about consumption	Have highest level of socio-oriented communication and medium level of concept-oriented communication with children	Have medium level of socio-oriented and concept-oriented communication with children	Have lowest level of socio-oriented communication and medium level of concept-oriented communication with children
Level of co-viewing	Occasionally watch TV with children	Occasionally watch TV with children; co-view more often than parents with children at perceptual stage	Occasionally watch TV with children; co-view more often than parents with children at analytical stage
Discuss with children about commercials	Seldom do so	Seldom do so	Seldom do so
Control of television viewing	High level of control	High level of control	High level of control
Perceived parental influence on children's attitudes toward TV advertising	Perceived they have some influence	Perceived they have some influence	Perceived they have some influence
Attitudes toward television advertising	Negative	Negative	Negative
Attitudes toward children's advertising	Negative	Negative; but not as strong as parents with children at perceptual stage	Negative; but not as strong as parents with children at analytical stage

Conclusions about children's and parents perception of TV advertising

Tables 10-1 and 10-2 have attempted to summarize the many findings in the book about kids' and parents' perceptions of TV advertising. Some basic conclusions can be drawn from them.

- Chinese children's development of understanding of TV commercials and their purposes mirrors the development of their cognitive abilities. That is, there is not much understanding of commercials and their purposes in the early years, but with the advent of the 100-month line, ages 8–9, children demonstrate some basic understanding. And when they reach the reflective stage at around age 12, they have a good grasp of understanding of what is TV advertising and its purposes. (The fact that very young children show an understanding of why TV stations broadcast commercials — an exception to children's development of understanding of commercials — may be a function of our research techniques. Teachers read out the possible answers, and they may have unknowingly emphasized "to make money." And it may be possible, also, that the children were parroting what is heard so often in new China — make money!)

- Since the very young children really do not understand TV commercials, they tend to see them as truthful until they reach the 100-month line at which time they have the ability to evaluate them more closely on their own and they judge some as truthful and some as untruthful.

- While some of the young children report liking some commercials, once they can make judgements about them — at around 100 months — they see them in a neutral light. At most they like informative ads including the PSAs. They do not see much of a link between advertising and brands.

- Overall, it appears that Chinese children are not emotionally involved with advertising; it does not seem to consume them or their mind-time. It seems not to be a major matter in their lives. It is probably not a frequent topic of conversation among them, and certainly not within the family. When our research procedures encourage them to talk about advertising, they do. But only when asked, and then they may select socially desirable answers. The plain fact of the matter is that there are other much more important impingements in Chinese children's lives than advertising — their studies, their parents' pressures on them to succeed, their teachers' requirements, their friends demands, their personal goals, fears, and worries.

• The parents in this study grew up when there was very little advertising and have seen it flourish. Today, they tend to mistrust it, perhaps see it as a capitalistic tool to make sales of products that may not be worthy of praise. The parents are very busy — probably both work — and take little time for TV viewing with their children and little time to talk about it. They are generally negative about TV ads, about TV ads that target their children, and probably pass on this thinking to their children. They really do not want their children viewing TV or responding to TV ads. TV is generally seen as a distraction from the children's studies. All in all, the Chinese households of today do not hold TV advertising in high regard. It is not a welcomed guest in their households, having built a reputation for dishonesty and mistargeting of messages — adults' messages often go to children.

A final summary and some major implications for advertisers and policy makers

The authors and researchers of this material feel blessed to have been able to conduct so much research on a topic that needs it so badly. What is presented to the reader here is the results of two years of work of a research team dedicated to ferreting out the facts regarding advertising on television that targets Chinese kids. We are proud to say that nowhere does this information exist or has ever existed. But we feel equally disappointed in the results in the sense that what they show is that most of the advertising that children receive adjacent to their programs that they are permitted to watch within very limited times is *not* intended for them and therefore could be misleading and certainly undesirable in the eyes of their parents and grandparents. Even the government recently found it necessary to place a brief moratorium on advertising on TV for medical products and services because they are so blatantly dishonest. The net outcome is that while children develop an understanding of advertising and its goals by the time they are 8 to 9-year-old, both children and parents do not like TV advertising very much, do not trust much of it, do not see it enhancing brands, and therefore the children (and parents too) pay little attention to it. This means that advertising to the current generation of children and parents is not very effective, that advertisers are not getting what they pay for.

Based on the voluminous findings that are summarized in Tables 10-1 and 10-2, along with the in-depth experience in the field of advertisings and children's consumer behavior possessed by the authors/researchers, the following implications are noted.

- Media education is a must for children. The advertising industry, along with the broadcasting industry, needs to get together with the education system and introduce some teaching modules for elementary school children. These classroom efforts, usually termed, consumer education, will help children (and their families) to understand how media function, how media and advertising work together, the nature and purposes of advertising, and the role of consumers — children and their parents — in all this.

- Separately, the advertising industry needs to start a public relations program for itself. It needs to sell itself to the public. It is its own worst enemy, producing lots of dishonest and poorly executed advertising, letting it be presented in the wrong time slots, and thus causing parents to express negative opinions about it to their children. The fact that advertising is generally mistrusted by this generation of kids, given little attention by them, and liked very little, is a function of the advertisers, not of consumers. Advertising must repair its bad image among Chinese consumers if it is to become acceptable and meet its goals. It apparently does not benefit the brands it presents to children.

- Advertisers must work closely with television broadcasters so that properly developed advertising messages are reaching their target. Currently, most of the advertising that surrounds children's programming is for adult products. Needless to say, this is often offensive to parents, and at least confusing and boring to children. Broadcasters must set aside the time slots where children are the primary audience for presenting products and services that target children, perhaps children and their parents. Advertisers of products for children must contract for these time slots and fill them with messages that are suitable for children.

- Commercials that target children must be crafted so that they appeal to children and their parents, probably in this order. It is a basic principle of marketing and advertising that the satisfaction of the needs and wants of the target audience should be the focus of the commercials — of the advertiser and the broadcaster. For example, children are particularly in need of play, but their parents prefer they spend their time learning. Thus, products and messages that practice "edutainment," that educate and entertain, are likely to be appropriate and acceptable to both.

- At the retail level sellers should be aware of those products and brands that are advertised to children and their families, and attempt to insure that the particular products meet their claims. Retailers should not be "partners in crime," in the sense they turn their heads to the false claims made by some advertisers. But they instead should foster a good, long-lasting relationship with producers based on brand integrity. This means conferring with producers who practice questionable advertising, and if necessary, not carrying their products. This is a basic responsibility to the customers of the stores.

- As for the legal environment of advertising to children, there needs to be a review of the regulations and self-regulations by objective and qualified people. It appears that separate rules and laws governing children's advertising need to be developed in China that take into consideration the lack of defenses and experience of children. The mere fact that young children trust advertising while older children do not begs for regulation that protects the younger children. Public records show that repeatedly dishonest advertising is practiced. Whatever regulations are now in force need to be changed, or the regulators need to be changed. Of course, such proper law making will only improve the image of advertising — the bad image of advertising. So, the advertising industry should support, even seek, such actions.

- Parents should complain about the inappropriate nature of commercials that reach their children. They should complain to the proper authorities, but also to television stations that air the inappropriate ads. Consumer rights are still not important to the business community in China, so parents must try harder, shout louder. They should also try to organize into consumer advocacy organizations that give them more clout, and take their complaints directly to advertisers in the name of the organizations. An advertiser might not listen to one consumer but will listen to a group of consumers. Chances are the government will also.

Bibliography

ACNielsen Media International. (2000). China-Gross Advertising Expenditure 1993–1999. *Asiacom, 6,* 10.

Alwitt, L., & Prabhaker, P. R. (1992). Functional and Belief Dimensions of Attitudes to Television Advertising: Implication for Copytesting. *Journal of Advertising Research, September/October,* 30–42.

Asia Law and Practice Limited. (1994). PRC, Advertising Law. In *Encyclopedia of Chinese Law Volume II* (pp. 153–156). Hong Kong: Asia Law and Practice Limited.

Atkin, C. K. (1975). *Effects of Television Advertising on Children: First Year Experimental Evidence, Report No. 1.* East Lansing: Michigan State University, Department of Communication.

Atkin, C. K. (1982). Television Advertising and Socialization to Consumer Roles. In K. Pearl, et al. (Eds.), *Television and Behaviour: Ten Years of Scientific Progress and Implications for the Eighties* (pp. 191–200). Rockville, MD: US Department of Health and Human Services.

Ban, W. (2002). State Administration of Industry and Commerce, Shanghai Yangpu Advertising Censorship Division. Personal Interview. October 23.

Bauer, R., & Greyser, S. (1968). *Advertising in America: The Consumer View.* Boston, MA: Harvard University Press.

Bearden, W. O., Jesse, E. T., & Robert, R. W. (1979). Family Income Effects on Measurement of Children's Attitudes toward Television Commercials. *Journal of Consumer Research, 6*(December), 308–311.

Bechtel, R. B., Achelpohl, C., & Akers, R. (1972). Correlates between Observed Behaviour and Questionnaire Responses on Television Viewing. In E. Rubinstein, G. A. Comstock & J. P. Murray (Eds.), *Television and Social Behavior* (Vol. 4, pp. 274–344). Washington, DC: US Government Printing Office.

Belk, R., Mayer, R., & Driscoll, A. (1984). Children's Recognition of Consumption Symbolism in Children's Products. *Journal of Consumer Research, 10,* 386–397.

Bever, T. G., Martin, L. S., Barbara, B., & Thomas, G. J. (1975). Young Viewers'

Troubling Response to TV Ads. *Harvard Business Review, 53*(November-December), 109–120.

Blosser, B. J., & Roberts, D. F. (1985). Age Differences in Children's Perceptions of Message Intent. *Communication Research, 12*(4), 455–484.

Bond, M. H. (1991). *Beyond Chinese Face: Insights from Psychology*. Hong Kong: Oxford University Press.

Boush, D. M., Friestad, M., & Rose, G. M. (1994). Adolescent Skepticism toward TV Advertising and Knowledge of Advertiser Tactics. *Journal of Consumer Research, 21*(June), 165–175.

Bu, W. (1998). Children Programming: Who's the Target? *Journalism and Communication Research (Xin wen yu chuan bo yan jiu), 5*(2), 13–24. (In Chinese).

Bu, W. (2001). *The Influence of Mass Media on Children (Da zhong chuan mei dui er tong de ying xiang)*. Beijing: Xinhua Publishing House. (In Chinese).

CCTV website. (2002). Retrieved December 15, from http://www.cctv.com

Chadwick, J. (1997). Navigating through China's New Advertising Law: The Role of Marketing Research. *International Journal of Advertising, 16*(4), 284–294.

Chan, K. (1997). Television Advertising Regulation and Public Opinions in China and Hong Kong (Zhong Gang dian shi guang gao guan li yu shi min yi jian). In T. M. Chan, L. Chu & C. D. Poon (Eds.), *Mass Communication and Market Economy (Da zhong chuan bo yu shi chang jing ji)*. Hong Kong: Lu Feng Society. (In Chinese).

Chan, K. (1998). Chinese Consumers' Medical Decisions and Attitudes toward Pharmaceutical Advertising. *Journal of International Consumer Marketing, 10*(4), 49–68.

Chan, K. (2000). Hong Kong Children's Understanding of Television Advertising. *Journal of Marketing Communications, 6*(1), 37–52.

Chan, K. (2001). Children's Perceived Truthfulness of Television Advertising and Parental Influence: A Hong Kong Study. In M. C. Gilly & J. Meyers-Levy (Eds.), *Advances in Consumer Research* (Vol. 28, pp. 207–212). Valdosta, GA: Associations for Consumer Research.

Chan, K., & McNeal, J. U. (2002). Children's Perceptions of Television Advertising in Urban China. *International Journal of Advertising and Marketing to Children, 3*(3), 69–79.

Chao, R. K., & Sue, S. (1996). Chinese Parental Influence and Their Children's School Success: A Paradox in the Literature on Parenting Styles. In S. Lau (Ed.), *Growing up the Chinese Way* (pp. 94–120). Hong Kong: The Chinese University Press.

Cheng, H. (1996). Advertising in China: A Socialist Experiment. In K. T.

Frith (Ed.), *Advertising in Asia: Communication, Culture and Consumption* (pp. 73–102). Ames, IA: Iowa State University Press.

Cheng, H. (1997a). Holding up Half of the Sky? A Sociocultural Comparison of Gender-role Portrayals in Chinese and US Advertising. *International Journal of Advertising, 16*(4), 295–319.

Cheng, H. (1997b). Toward an Understanding of Cultural Values Manifest in Advertising: A Content Analysis of Chinese Television Commercials in 1990 and 1995. *Journalism & Mass Communication Quarterly, 74*(4), 773–796.

Cheng, H. (2000). China: Advertising Yesterday and Today. In J. P. Jones (Ed.), *International Advertising: Realities and Myths* (pp. 255–284). Thousand Oaks, CA: Sage.

Cheng, H. (2003). *Advertising Law Implementation in China: A Six-"tions" Analysis of Illegal Cases.* Proceedings of the 2003 Asia Pacific Conference of the American Academy of Advertising, Japan, 3–11.

Children's Advertising Review Unit. (2003). *Self-Regulatory Guidelines for Children's Advertising: Guidelines for Interactive Electronic Media (e.g. Internet and Online Services).* Retrieved April 9, from http://www.caru.org/carusubpgs/guidepg.asp

China Advertising (Zhongguo guanggao). (1994). Some Regulations on Experimental Advertising Agency System (Trial Implement). *51*, 3. (In Chinese).

China Advertising Association. (2002). *Self-regulatory Guidelines for Spiritual Civilization in Advertising (Guang gao xuan chuan jing shen wen ming zi lu gui ze).* Retrieved December 20, from http://www.cnad.com/ggfg/ggfg01/1009.htm (In Chinese).

China Advertising Yearbook (Zhong guo guang gao nian jian). (2001). *Basic Facts of National Advertising Monitoring and Management in 2000 (2000 nian quan guo guang gao jian du guan li ji ben qing kuang).* Beijing: Xinhua Publishing House. (In Chinese).

China Audio Visual and Film Net (Zhong guo yin xiang dian ying wang). (2002). *Publication Statistics of Audio Visual Products in year 2001 (2001 yin xiang dian zi zhi pin chu ban fa hang tong ji).* Retrieved 17 December, from http://av.ccnt.com.cn (In Chinese).

China Business (Zhong guo jing ying bao). (2001). China Consumer Association Publishes Fake Ads (Zhong xia xie gong bu xu jia guang gao). August 23. (In Chinese).

China Infobank. (2003). *China Statistical Yearbook 2002.* Retrieved January 13, from http://www.chinainfobank.com (In Chinese).

China Media Net (Zhong hua chuan mei wang). (2002a). *Hunan Province Stops All Media from Showing Medical Ads (Wei fa guang gao you xiao zhang*

Hu nan zan jin ge mei ti fa bu yi yao guang gao). Retrieved February 14, from http://www.mediafriend.com/news/ad229.html (In Chinese).

China Media Net (Zhong hua chuan mei wang). (2002b). *The State Administration for Industry and Commerce of Beijing Reported that Nearly 100% of the Recent Medical Ads Had Violated the Regulations (Bei jing gong shang ju fa bu: jin qi yi liao guang gao wei fa lu gao da 100%).* Retrieved April 18, from http://www.mediafriend.com/news/ad285.html (In Chinese).

Chinese Academy of Social Sciences. (2000). An Assessment of Children's TV Programmes in the People's Republic of China. In G. Hogan (Ed.), *Growing Up With TV* (pp. 12–47). Singapore: Asian Media Information and Communication Centre.

Chinese Consumer Newspaper (Zhong guo xiao fei zhe bao). (1994). A Long Way toward Protecting the Consumers, July 4, p. 1. (In Chinese).

Collins, J. (1990). Television and Primary School Children in Northern Ireland, The Impact of Advertising. *Journal of Educational Television, 16,* 31–39.

Crosby, L. A., & Grossbart, S. (1984). Parental Style Segments and Concern about Children Food Advertising. In J. H. Leigh & Jr C.R. Martin (Eds.), *Current Issues in Research in Advertising* (pp. 53–63). Ann Arbor, MI: Division of Research, Graduate School of Business Administration, University of Michigan.

CVSC-TNS Research. (2002). *CCTV-1 Quarter Hour Rating, January to March 2002, Age Group 4–14.* Obtained from the company.

Davis, D. S., & Sensenbrenner, J. S. (2000). Commercializing Childhood: Parental Purchases for Shanghai's Only Child. In D. S. Davis (Ed.), *The Consumer Revolution in Urban China* (pp. 54–79). Berkeley, CA: University of California Press.

Domino, G. (1992). Cooperation and Competition in Chinese and American Children. *Journal of Cross-Cultural Psychology, 23*(4), 456–467.

Eckholm, E. (2002). Desire for Sons Drives Use of Prenatal Scans in China. *The New York Times,* June 21, p. A23.

Ekblad, S. (1986). Relationships between Child-rearing Practices and Primary School Children's Functional Adjustment in the People's Republic of China. *Scandinavian Journal of Psychology, 21,* 697–715.

Fan, L. (2001). Review of the China Advertising Industry in 2000. *China Advertising (Zhongguo guanggao), 2*(June), 70–76. (In Chinese).

Friestad, M., & Wright, P. (1994). The Persuasion Knowledge Model: How People Cope with Persuasion Attempts. *Journal of Consumer Research, 21* (June), 1–31.

Furnham, A. (2000). *Children and Advertising: The Allegations and the Evidence.* London: The Social Affairs Unit.

Goll, S. D. (1995). Markeing: China's (Only) Children Get the Royal Treatment. *The Asia Wall Street Journal*, February 8, p. B1.

Greenberg, B. S., Fazal, S., & Wober, M. (1986). *Children's Views on Advertising (Research Report)*. London: Independent Broadcasting Authority.

Greenberg, B. S., Li, H., Ku, L., & Wang, J. (1991). Young People and Mass Media in China. *Asian Journal of Communication, 1*(2), 122–142

Guest, L. P. (1955). Brand Loyalty: Twelve Years Later. *Journal of Applied Psychology, 39*(December), 405–408.

Gunter, B., & McAleer, J. (1997). *Children and Advertising* (2nd ed.). London: Routledge.

Guo, Y. (2000). Food and Family Relations: The Generation Gap at the Table. In J. Jing (Ed.), *Feeding China's Little Emperors: Food, Children, and Social Change* (pp. 94–113). CA: Stanford University Press.

Ha, L. (1996). Concerns about Advertising Practices in a Developing Country: An Examination of China's New Advertising Regulations. *International Journal of Advertising, 15*, 91–102.

Hatfield, S. (2002). China Shuts Down Drug Ads as It Copes with Ad Explosion. *Advertising Age*, February 4, p. 16.

Henriksen, L. (1997). *Children's Understanding of the Purposes of Advertising*. Paper presented at the Mass Communication Division, International Communication Association Annual Meeting, Montreal.

Ho, D. (1976). On the Concept of Face. *American Journal of Sociology, 81*(4), 867–884.

Ho, D. (1989). Continuity and Variation in Chinese Patterns of Socialization. *Journal of Marriage and the Family, 51*, 149–163.

Hofstede, G. (1980). *Culture's Consequences: International Differences in Work-related Values*. Newbury Park, CA: Sage.

Hofstede, G. (1983). National Culture in Four Dimensions. *International Studies of Management and Organization, 13*(2), 46–74.

Hofstede, G. (1991). *Culture and Organization: Software of the Mind*. London: McGraw-Hill.

Hofstede, G. (1994). Management Scientists are Humans. *Management Science, 40*(January), 4–13.

Hofstede, G. (1998). *Masculinity and Femininity: The Taboo Dimension of National Cultures*. Thousand Oaks, CA: Sage.

Hsu, F. L. L. (1981). *American and Chinese: Passage to Differences* (3rd ed.). Honolulu: University Press of Hawaii.

International Chamber of Commerce. (2002). *ICC International Code of Advertising Practice (1997 Edition)*. Retrieved April 1, from http://www. itcilo.it/english/actrav/telearn/global/ilo/guide/iccadv.htm

Itoh, F., & Taylor, C. M. (1981). A Comparison of Childrearing Expectations of Parents in Japan and the United States. *Journal of Comparative Family Studies, 12*(4), 449–460.

Ji, M. F., & McNeal, J. U. (2001). How Chinese Children's Commercials Differ from Those of the United States: A Content Analysis. *Journal of Advertising, 30*(3), 79–92.

Jie fang Daily (Jie fang bao). (2002). *The State Administration for Industry and Commerce is Going to Stop All the Media from Showing Medical Ads for a Longer Time Nationally (Guo jia gong shang ju ni zai quan guo fan wei nei jiao chang shi jian jin fa yi liao guang gao).* April 19, from http://www.mediafriend.com/news/ad284.html (In Chinese).

John, D. R. (1999). Consumer Socialization of Children: A Retrospective Look at Twenty-five Years of Research. *Journal of Consumer Research, 26* (December), 183–213.

Kelly, J. L., & Tseng, H. M. (1992). Cultural Differences in Child Rearing: A Comparison of Immigrant Chinese and Caucasian American Mothers. *Journal of Cross-cultural Psychology, 23*(4), 444–455.

Kovarik, L. (2001). *Sophisticated Mainland Chinese Tire of "Boring" Ads.* Unpublished survey results. Hong Kong: Leo Burnett Hong Kong.

Kwan, Y. K., Ho, Y. N., & Cragin, J. P. (1983). Contemporary Advertising Attitudes and Practices among Executives in the People's Republic of China. *Journal of the Marketing Research Society, 25*(January), 59–71.

Lei, T. (1993). *Metzger's Model for the Modern Moral Man.* Paper presented at the International Conference on Moral and Civic Education, November, Hong Kong.

Leiss, W., Kline, S., & Jhally, S. (1990). *Social Communication in Advertising: Persons, Products and Images of Well-Being* (2nd ed.). Ontario: Nelson Canada.

Li, D., & Gallup, A. M. (1995). In Search of the Chinese Consumer. *The China Business Review, September-October,* 19–22.

Liang, K., & Jacobs, L. (1994). China's Advertising Agencies: Problems and Relations. *International Journal of Advertising, 13*(3), 205–215.

Lichtenberger, J. (1986). *Advertising Compliance Law: Handbook for Marketing Professionals and Their Counsel.* New York: Quorum Books.

Lindquist, J. D. (1978). Children's Attitudes toward Advertising on Television and Radio and in Children's Magazines and Comic Books. In W. L. Wilkie (Ed.), *Advances in Consumer Research* (Vol. 6, pp. 407–412). Ann Arbor, MI: Association for Consumer Research.

Liu, H. Y., & Liu, Y. Z. (1996). Single Child and the Forecast of their Family Profile (Du sheng zi nu ji qi wei lai hun yin jie guo). *Population Science of China (Zhong guo ren kou ke xue), 54,* 33–37. (In Chinese).

Liu, W. L. (2002). Advertising in China: Product Branding and Beyond. *Corporate Communications: An International Journal, 7*(2), 117–125.

Luo, W. (2000). Watch out for Children Advertising. *China Women Daily (Zhong guo fu nu bao)*, November 13. (In Chinese).

Lutz, R. (1975). Measurement and Diagnosis of Student Attitudes toward a Career in Advertising. *Journal of Advertising, 4*(3, Summer), 36–40.

Lu zhong News (*Lu zhong chen bao*). (2002). *A Shandong Couple Was Fined 500 Thousand Dollars due to Breaking of the Family Planning Policy (Shang dong yi dui fu fu wei fan ji hua sheng yu zheng ce chao sheng bei zheng 50 wan).* September 6, from http://news.xinhuanet.com/newscenter/2002-09/06/content_552174.htm (In Chinese).

Macklin, M. C. (1987). Preschoolers' Understanding of the Informational Function of Television Advertising. *Journal of Consumer Research, 14* (September), 229–239.

Mallalieu, L., Palan, K., & Laczniak, R. (2002). *Examining Children's Cognitive Abilities in an Advertising Context: Differences in Breadth and Depth across Age Groups.* Paper presented at the Association for Consumer Research Annual Conference, Atlanta.

Mangleburg, T. F., & Terry, B. (1998). *Socialization and Adolescents' Skepticism toward Advertising* (Working paper). Fort Lauderdale, 33301: College of Business, Florida Atlantic University.

Martin, M. C., & James, W. G. (1997). Stuck in the Model Trap: The Effects of Beautiful Models in Ads on Female Pre-adolescents and Adolescents. *Journal of Advertising, 26*(Summer), 19–33.

McLeod, J., Fitzpatrick, M., Glynn, C., & Fallis, S. (1982). Television and Social Relations: Family Influences and Consequences for Interpersonal Behavior. In E. A. K. Pearl (Ed.), *Television and Behaviour: Ten Years of Scientific Progress and Implications for the Eighties* (pp. 272–286). Rockville, MD: US Department of Health and Human Services.

McNeal, J. U. (1987). *Children as Consumers: Insights and Implications.* Lexington, MA: Lexington Books.

McNeal, J. U. (1991). Planning Priorities for Marketing to Children. *Journal of Business Strategy, May/June*, 12–15.

McNeal, J. U. (1992). *Kids as Customers: A Handbook of Marketing to Children.* Lexington, MA: Lexington Books.

McNeal, J. U. (1993). Charting the Consumer Trainee. *Food and Beverage Marketing*, December, 18–20.

McNeal, J. U. (1999). *The Kids Market: Myths and Realities.* Ithaca, NY: Paramount Market Publishers.

McNeal, J. U., & Ji, M. F. (1996). Children's Influence on Chinese Families'

Newfound Leisure Time and Its Marketing Implications. *Asia Pacific Journal of Marketing and Logistics, 8*(3), 32–57.

McNeal, J. U., & Ji, M. F. (1998). The Role of Mass Media in the Consumer Socialization of Chinese Children. In K. Hung & K. Monroe (Eds.), *Asia Pacific Advances in Consumer Research* (Vol. 3, pp. 6–12). Valdosta, GA: Association for Consumer Research.

McNeal, J. U., & Ji, M. F. (1999). Chinese Children as Consumers: An Analysis of their New Product Information Sources. *Journal of Consumer Marketing, 16*(4), 345–364.

McNeal, J. U., & Wu, S. (1995). Consumer Choices are Child's Play in China. *The Asia Wall Street Journal*, October 23, p. 14.

McNeal, J. U., & Yeh, C. H. (1997). Development of Consumer Behaviour Patterns among Chinese Children. *Journal of Consumer Marketing, 14*(1), 45–59.

McNeal, J. U., & Yeh, C. H. (2003). Consumer Behaviour of Chinese Children, 1995–2002. *Journal of Consumer Marketing, forthcoming.*

McNeal, J. U., & Zhang, H. (2000). Chinese Children's Consumer Behaviour: A Review. *Advertising & Marketing to Children, March/April*, 31–37.

Meringoff, L. K., & Lesser, G. S. (1980). Children's Ability to Distinguish Television Commercials from Program Material. In R. P. Adler, G. S. Lesser, L. K. Meringoff, T. S. Robertson, J. R. Rossiter & S. Ward (Eds.), *The Effects of Television Advertising on Children* (pp. 29–42). Lexington, MA: Lexington Books.

Metzger, T. (1992). *The Thoughts of Tang Chun-I (1909–1978): A Preliminary Response.* Paper presented at the Proceedings of the International Conference on Tang's Thoughts, Fa-tzu, Hong Kong.

Meyer, T. P., Donohue, T. R., & Henke, L. L. (1978). How Black Kids See TV Commercials. *Journal of Advertising Research, 18*(October), 51–58.

Miao, S. (1995). Confusion Reigns: China's Agencies Struggle to Tame Fierce New Rules. *Adweek, 36*(April 17), 26–28.

Mittal, B. (1994). Public Assessment of TV Advertising: Faint Praise and Harsh Criticism. *Journal of Advertising Research, January/February*, 35–53.

Modern Advertising (Xian dai guang gao). (2001). Alert to Advertising, *2*, 22–25. (In Chinese).

Moore, R., & Stephens, L. (1975). Some Communication and Demographic Determinants of Adolescent Consumer Learning. *Journal of Consumer Research, 2*(September), 80–92.

Moore-Shay, E. S., & Lutz, R. J. (1997). *Kids' Consumption: How Do Children Perceive the Relationships between Advertisements and Products* (Working paper). Urbana-Champaign, 61820: Office of Research, College of Commerce and Business Administration, University of Illinois.

Moschis, G. P. (1987). *Consumer Socialization: A Life-cycle Perspective.* Lexington, MA: Lexington Books.

Moschis, G. P., & Churchill, G. A., Jr. (1978). Consumer Socialization: A Theoretical and Empirical Analysis. *Journal of Marketing Research, 15* (November), 599–609.

Moschis, G. P., & Moore, R. L. (1982). A Longitudinal Study of Television Advertising Effects. *Journal of Consumer Research, 9*, 279–286.

Mosher, S. W. (2001). *Population Control in China* (Congressional testimony): President, Population Research Institute, Federal Document Clearing House, Inc.

Nippold, M. A., Cuyler, J. S., & Braunbeck-Price, R. (1988). Explanation of Ambiguous Advertisements: A Developmental Study with Children and Adolescents. *Journal of Speech and Hearing Research, 31*, 466–474.

Oates, C., Blades, M., & Gunter, B. (2002). Children and Television Advertising: When Do They Understand Persuasive Intent? *Journal of Consumer Behaviour, 1*(3), 238–245.

O'Guinn, T. C., & Shrum, L. J. (1997). The Role of Television in the Construction of Consumer Reality. *Journal of Consumer Research, 23*(March), 278–294.

O'Hanlon, T. (2000). Building a "Kid Contract" with Chinese Kids: Part II. *International Journal of Advertising and Marketing to Children, 2*(3), 205–209.

Paget, K. F., Kritt, D., & Bergemann, L. (1984). Understanding Strategic Interactions in Television Commercials: A Developmental Study. *Journal of Applied Developmental Psychology, 5* (April–June), 145–161.

Piaget, J. (1970). The Stages of the Intellectual Development of the Child. In P. H. Mussen, J. J. Conger & J. Kagan (Eds.), *Readings in Child Development and Personality* (pp. 291–298). New York: Harper and Row.

Pollay, R. W., & Mittal, B. (1993). Here's the Beef: Factors, Determinants, and Segments in Consumer Criticism of Advertising. *Journal of Marketing, 57*(3), 99–114.

Poole, T. (1996). Engineers of the Soul Try to Fill China's Moral Vacuum. *South China Morning Post,* pp. 12, September 21.

Population Reference Bureau. (2003). Retrieved April 11, from http://prb.org

Power, T. G., Kobayashi-Winata, H., & Kelley, M. L. (1992). Childrearing Patterns in Japan and the United States: A Cluster Analytic Study. *International Journal of Behavioural Development, 1*(2), 185–205.

Riffe, D., Lacy, S., & Fico, F. G. (1998). *Analyzing Media Messages: Using*

Quantitative Content Analysis in Research. Mahwah, NJ: Lawrence Erlbaum Associates.

Robertson, T. S., & Rossiter, J. R. (1974). Children and Commercial Persuasion: An Attribution Theory Analysis. *Journal of Consumer Research, 1*(June), 13–20.

Robertson, T. S., Ward, S., Gatignon, H., & Klees, D. M. (1989). Advertising and Children: A Cross-cultural Study. *Communication Research, 16*(August), 459–485.

Rose, G. M., Bush, V. D., & Kahle, L. (1998). The Influence of Family Communication Patterns on Parental Reactions toward Advertising: A Cross-national Examination. *Journal of Advertising, 27*(4), 71–85.

Rossiter, J. R. (1977). Reliability of a Short Test Measuring Children's Attitudes towards TV Commercials. *Journal of Consumer Research, 3*(March), 179–184.

Rossiter, J. R., & Robertson, T. S. (1976). Canonical Analysis of Developmental, Social, and Experiential Factors in Children's Comprehension of Television Advertising. *Journal of Genetic Psychology, 129*(December), 317–327.

Rubin, R. S. (1974). The Effects of Cognitive Development on Children's Response to Television Advertising. *Journal of Business Research, 2*(October), 409–419.

Russell, C. A. (2002). Investigating the Effectiveness of Product Placements in Television Shows: The Role of Modality and Plot Connection Congruence on Brand Memory and Attitude. *Journal of Consumer Research, 29*(3), 293–305.

Sdinfo Net (2002). *Southern Weekend Disclose the Four Deceiving Techniques used by "Zhung hua ling zhi bao."* Retrieved May 31, from http://news.sdinfo.net/72355561689055232/20020531/1036582.shtml (In Chinese).

Selman, R. L. (1980). *The Growth of Interpersonal Understanding*. New York: Academic Press.

Semenik, R. J., Zhou, N., & Moor, W. L. (1986). Chinese Managers' Attitudes toward Advertising in General. *Journal of Advertising, 15*(4), 56–62.

Shao, A., & Herbig, P. (1994). Marketing Implications of China's Little Emperors. *Review of Business, 16*(Summer/Fall), 16–20.

Shavitt, S., Lowrey, P., & Haefner, J. (1998). Public Attitudes toward Advertising: More Favorable than You Might Think. *Journal of Advertising Research, 38*(4), 7–22.

Shim, S., Snyder, L., & Gehrt, K. C. (1995). Parents' Perception Regarding Children's Use of Clothing Evaluative Criteria: An Exploratory Study from the Consumer Socialization Process Perspective. In F. R. Kardes & M. Sujan (Eds.), *Advances in Consumer Research* (Vol. 22, pp. 628–632). Ann Arbor, MI: Association for Consumer Research.

Soley, L. C., & Reid, L. N. (1984). *When Parents Control Children's TV Viewing and Product Choice: Testing the Attitudinal Defenses.* Paper presented at the Marketing Comes of Age: Proceedings of the Annual Meeting of the Southern Marketing Association, Boca Raton, FL.

Stander, V., & Jensen, L. (1993). The Relationship of Value Orientation to Moral Cognition: Gender and Cultural Differences in the United States and China Explored. *Journal of Cross-cultural Psychology, 24*(1), 42–52.

State Administration for Industry and Commerce and State Planning Committee. (1993a). *An Outline on Speeding-up the Development of Advertising.*

State Administration for Industry and Commerce and State Planning Committee. (1993b). *The Interim Advertising Censorship Standards.*

Stephens, N., & Stutts, M. A. (1982). Preschoolers' Ability to Distinguish Between Television Programming and Commercials. *Journal of Advertising, 11*(2), 16–26.

Sutherland, M., & Galloway, J. (1981). Role of Advertising: Persuasion or Agenda Setting. *Journal of Advertising Research, 21*(October), 25–29.

Ward, S. (1972). Children's Reactions to Commercials. *Journal of Advertising Research, 12*(April), 37–45.

Ward, S. (1974). Consumer Socialization. *Journal of Consumer Research, 1* (September), 1–14.

Ward, S., Levinson, D., & Wackman, D. B. (1972). Children's Attention to Television Advertising. In *Television and Social Behaviour* (Vol. 4, pp. 491–516). Washington, DC: Government Printer Office.

Ward, S., & Wackman, D. B. (1973). Children's Information Processing of Television Advertising. In P. Clarke (Ed.), *New Models for Communication Research* (pp. 119–146). Beverly Hills, CA: Sage.

Ward, S., Wackman, D. B., & Wartella, E. (1977). *How Children Learn to Buy: The Development of Consumer Information Processing Skills.* Beverly Hills, CA: Sage.

Wartella, E., & Ettema, J. S. (1974). A Cognitive Developmental Study of Children's Attention to Television Commercials. *Communication Research, 1*(1), 44–69.

Watson, J. L. (2000). China's Big Mac Attack. *Foreign Affairs, 79*(3), 120–134.

Weber, I. G. (1999). Challenges Facing China's Television Advertising Industry in the Age of Spiritual Civilisation: An Industry Analysis. *International Journal of Advertising, 19*(2), 259–281.

Wei, R. (1997). Emerging Lifestyles in China and Consequences for Perception of Advertising, Buying Behaviour and Consumption Preferences. *International Journal of Advertising, 16,* 261–275.

Williams, J. E., & Best, D. L. (1990). *Measuring Sex Stereotypes*. Newbury Park, CA: Sage.

Wiseman, P. (1999). Tidal Wave of TV Ads Overwhelms Some Chinese Viewers Rebel against Blitz by Suing. *USA Today*, October 18.

Xinhua News Agency. (1995). China Bans Illegal Advertisements. March 22.

Xinhua News Agency. (1998). World's Largest Ad Market. September 27.

Xinhua News Agency. (2000). China's Commerce Administration Praises Advertising law. December 22.

Xin kuai News (*Xin kuai bao*). (2002). *98% of the Medical Ads in Guangzhou Violate the Advertising Regulations (Guang zhou yi liao guang gao 98% wei fa)*. April 27, from http://www.mediafriend.com/news/ad278.html (In Chinese).

Xu, B. (1990). *Marketing to China: One Billion New Customers*. Lincolnwood, IL: NTC Business Books.

Xu, B. (1992). Reaching the Chinese Consumer. *The China Business Review, 19*(November–December), 36–42.

Yang, C. K. (1959). *The Chinese Family in the Communist Revolution*. Cambridge, MA: MIT Press.

Yau, O. (1988). Chinese Cultural Values: Their Dimensions and Marketing Implications. *European Journal of Marketing, 22*(5), 44–57.

Yau, O. (1994). *Consumer Behaviour in China: Consumer Satisfaction and Cultural Values*. New York, NY: Routledge.

Young, B. M. (2000). The Child's Understanding of Promotional Communication. *International Journal of Advertising and Marketing to Children, 2*(3), 191–203.

Zeng, Y. (2002). A Demographic Analysis of Family Households in China, 1982–1995. *Journal of Comparative Family Studies, 33*(1), 15–34.

Zhang, L. T. (2001). *Advertising Laws and Regulations: Case Studies (Guang gao fa gui an li jiao cheng)*. Shanghai: Shanghai University Press. (In Chinese).

Zhang, W. (1999). Implementation of State Family Planning Programmes in a Northern Chinese Village. *The China Quarterly, 157*, 202–230.

Zhang, Y., & Gelb, B. D. (1996). Matching Advertising Appeals to Culture: The Influence of Products' Use Conditions. *Journal of Advertising, 25*(3), 29–46.

Zhao, B. (1996). The Little Emperors' Small Screen: Parental Control and Children's Television Viewing in China. *Media, Culture & Society, 18*(4), 639–658.

Zhao, X., & Shen, F. (1995). Audience Reaction to Commercial Advertising in China in the 1980's. *International Journal of Advertising, 14*, 374–390.

Zhou, Y. (2001). *Children Advertising Causes Worries. Fu jian Daily (Fu jian ri bao). September 25,* from http://myhome.asia1.com.sg/special/newspapers/ 2001/09/fjdaily250901.html (In Chinese).

Zhu, N. (2000). *Advertising Law and Cases for Discussion (Guang gao fa shi li shuo).* Hunan: Hunan People's Press. (In Chinese).

Subject Index